The House Rules Committee

An advanced study in political science

The House Rules Committee

JAMES A. ROBINSON

Northwestern University

THE **BOBBS-MERRILL** COMPANY, INC.
A SUBSIDIARY OF HOWARD W. SAMS & CO., INC.
Publishers • INDIANAPOLIS • NEW YORK

Robert C. Wood
CONSULTING EDITOR
The Massachusetts Institute of Technology

Acknowledgments

This book consists largely of the analysis of documents of the Committee on Rules, access to which was cordially provided by Mr. T. M. Carruthers, Clerk; Mrs. Barbara Thornton, former Assistant Clerk; and Miss Mary Spencer Forrest, Assistant Clerk. Interpretation of these and other materials has been supplemented by a number of interviews with members of the Committee. To the Committee members and their staffs, I am deeply grateful for their continuing help.

At various stages, the whole manuscript was critically read by Professor Paul C. Bartholomew of the University of Notre Dame, Professor Richard C. Snyder of Northwestern University, Professor Robert C. Wood of The Massachusetts Institute of Technology, and my friend Jack Guthman, of Chicago. Their generous expenditure of time and care helped improve the final version immeasurably. In addition to receiving their counsel, I have benefited from conversations with other academic observers of the Committee, especially Dr. Robert L. Peabody of The Johns Hopkins University and my former student, Mont P. Hoyt.

Support for the research came through a University Fellowship from the Graduate School of Northwestern University, from a Congressional Fellowship of the American Political Science Association, and from the Illinois Center for Education in Politics.

For permission to revise, extend, and incorporate here portions of my earlier articles on the Committee, I am grateful to the editors and publishers of *The Western Political Quarterly; The Midwest Journal of Political Science;* The American Enterprise Institute's Special Legislative Analysis series; *The American Political Arena,* editor, Joseph R. Fiszman (Boston: Little, Brown & Co., 1962); *The Progressive;* and The Dorsey Press (*Congress and Foreign Policy-Making,* pp. 201-03). An early draft of this book was submitted as my doctoral dissertation at Northwestern University in 1957.

It is with sublime regret that I dedicate this book to one whose death deprived me and a generation of other former students at the University of Oklahoma of a thoughtful friend and academic mentor. H. V. Thornton was among the first to interest me in the study of legislatures; because he respected legislators, I like to think he would have appreciated this book.

To the memory of
H. V. THORNTON

Preface

The plan of this book is as follows. Chapter 1 assesses the power of the Rules Committee by considering the decisions of the House in which it participates; these decisions principally concern the agenda of the House. In addition, the chapter analyzes the base, means, and extent of the Committee's power with particular reference to the weight, scope, and domain of that power.

Chapter 2 is a more detailed consideration of the Committee's role in setting the agenda of the House, including the requests for hearings and for rules which it grants or denies. The Committee's role in arbitrating differences between legislative committees over procedural matters is also discussed, as is the House's record for accepting or rejecting the decisions of the Rules Committee.

Chapter 3 is devoted to the Committee's decisions regulating debate, through closed and open rules, through waivers of points of order, and through rules to dispose of differences between the House and Senate over the final form of a bill. The Committee's decisions about allocation of time for debate are also discussed.

Chapter 4 considers the historical developments and changes in the Committee's role, with emphasis on the House's expectations of the Committee as revealed in House reforms of 1910, 1949, and 1961. The special role and powers and personal performances of several of the chairmen are also analyzed. Chapter 5 examines the previous Congressional experience and the constituency backgrounds of members of the Committee and relates these two factors to their voting decisions, in an effort to show how an apprenticeship period, safe or competitive constituencies, and urban or rural residencies may affect members' decisions.

Chapter 6 discusses criticisms and proposed reforms of the Committee in terms of the doctrines of party responsibility and of legislative independence. In this chapter, I venture to offer a recommendation for a change in the Committee's role.

A word should be added about the time period for which detailed statistical data were collected. In most cases, intensive analysis of the Committee's record is reported for the period 1937-1962. However, owing to the availability of data, some tables are for shorter periods.

Contents

Acknowledgments   v
Preface   ix
Tables   xiii

1. THE POWER OF THE COMMITTEE   1

   The Calendars   3
   Special Legislative Days   6
   Special Rules   10
   SUMMARY   21

2. SETTING THE AGENDA   23

   Hearings Denied   23
   Rules Denied   25
   Arbitration of Committee Conflicts   30
   House Review of Rules Committee Decisions   33
   SUMMARY   41

3. REGULATING DEBATE AND ALLOCATING TIME   43

   Closed and Open Rules   43
   Waivers of Points of Order   47

Rules to Dispose of House-Senate Differences   51
Length of Time for Debate   53
SUMMARY   55

4. COMMITTEE ORGANIZATION AND COMMITTEE DECISIONS   57

Origins and Growth   58
The Revolt Against Cannon   60
The 21-Day Rule   63
"Packing" the Committee   71
The Chairman's Power   81

5. ORGANIZATIONAL EXPERIENCE, CONSTITUENCY
     BACKGROUNDS, AND COMMITTEE DECISIONS   89

Organizational Experience   92
Constituency Backgrounds   98
Consequences for Policy   103

6. PROPOSED REFORMS: PARTY RESPONSIBILITY VERSUS   111
     LEGISLATIVE INDEPENDENCE

Procedural Obstacle to Reform   113
Reforms to Promote Party Responsibility   114
Reforms to Promote Legislative Independence   121

Bibliography   129
Index   137

Tables

1 Parliamentary Means by Which Bills and Resolutions
   Pass the House   5
2 Use of Discharge Petition and Discharge Calendar
   to Consider Bills   6
3 Use of Calendar Wednesday to Bring Issues to the Floor   9
4 Subjects of Bills for Which Rules Committee Would Not
   Grant Rules: 80th to 86th Congresses   25
5 Bills for Whose Consideration Rules Were Defeated   38
6 Length of Time for Debate Under Open and Closed Rules   54
7 Frequency of Straight- and Cross-Party Committee Roll Calls   62
8 Number of the Members' Terms of Service in Which They
   Were Assigned to the Committee on Rules, 1937-62   93
9 Previous Committee Assignments of Members of
   Committee on Rules, 1937-62   97
10 Distribution by States of Membership of Committee on
   Rules, 1937-62   98
11 Regional Distribution of Membership of Committee on
   Rules, 1937-62   100
12 Urban-Rural Distribution of Members of Rules
   Committee, 1937-62   101
13 Safe-Competitive Character of Constituencies of Members
   of Committee on Rules, 1937-62   102
14 Party Unity Scores of Term Prior to Appointment, 1945-61   105

15 Party Unity Scores of Safe and Competitive Members,
   1945-62   106
16 Party Unity Scores of Urban and Rural Members,
   1945-62   107
17 Bipartisan Unity Scores and Competitiveness and Urbanism
   of Members' Constituencies, 1953-60   108

1

The Power
of the
Committee

politics is committee politics. In the House of Representatives twenty standing committees divide the thousands of bills introduced each year and assign them among another one hundred or more sub-committees.[1] When the full membership of the House considers a few of these for final deliberation and decision, it does so in the Committee of the Whole. Standing at the gateway to the Committee of the Whole and between it and the legislative committees is the

---

[1] For studies of other contemporary Congressional committees, see Holbert N. Carroll, *The House of Representatives and Foreign Affairs* (Pittsburgh: University of Pittsburgh Press, 1958), pp. 25-193; Charles O. Jones, *The Relationship of Congressional Committee Action to a Theory of Representation* (Ph.D. dissertation, University of Wisconsin, 1960); Jones, "Representation in Congress: The Case of the House Agriculture Committee," *American Political Science Review,* 55 (1961), 358-67; David N. Farnsworth, *The Senate Committee on Foreign Relations* (Urbana: University of Illinois Press, 1961); Richard F. Fenno, Jr., "The House Appropriations Committee as a Political System: The Problem of Integration," *American Political Science Review,* 56 (1962), 310-24.

On the committees that resolve differences between House and Senate on specific bills, see Gilbert Y. Steiner, *The Congressional Conference Committees: Seventieth to Eightieth Congresses* (Urbana: University of Illinois Press, 1951).

Committee on Rules, long recognized as one of the most important and powerful units in Congress.

A nineteenth-century member called the Committee a "dignified oligarchy," and Woodrow Wilson compared it to "a steering ministry,— without a ministry's public responsibility, and without a ministry's right to speak for both houses." More recently it has been called "the governing committee of the House," "the terrible twelve," and "the most powerful and the most irresponsible organ of the House." One writer credits it with having "more to say about the final legislative output than any other group on Capitol Hill." Its Chairman, regardless of personality, is said to be "one of the three outstanding leaders in the House," and a former Chairman once proclaimed that "in me reposes absolute obstructive powers."[2]

In the House of Representatives 435 members are in session approximately eight months each year to consider thousands of proposals for adoption as public policy. In the 84th Congress (1955-56) the House was presented with 14,104 bills and resolutions.[3] Assuming it had remained in session every minute for the full two years of its term, the House could have given seventy-five minutes to each bill and resolution. It is well known that many proposals that are placed in the "hopper" are not expected to pass, even by their sponsors, and it is admitted by Congressmen that they occasionally introduce measures they personally oppose. Nevertheless, some procedure is required to separate the chaff from the wheat, and to this end, in the second quarter of the nineteenth century, the House began to establish a series of standing, subject-matter committees to give pre-

[2] Woodrow Wilson, *Congressional Government* (New York: Meridian Books, 1956), pp. 87, 21; George B. Galloway, *The Legislative Process in Congress* (New York: Thomas Y. Crowell Company, 1953), p. 341; Henry F. and Katherine Pringle, "The 'Terrible Twelve' of Capitol Hill," *Saturday Evening Post* (June 19, 1954), 22 ff.; James McGregor Burns, *Congress on Trial: The Legislative Process and the Administrative State* (New York: Harper and Brothers, 1949), p. 56; Alan L. Otten, "Here's How 12 Men Control Congress," *Nation's Business* (February 1956), 33 ff.; Floyd M. Riddick, *The United States Congress: Organization and Procedure* (Manassas, Va.: National Capitol Publishers, Inc., 1949), pp. 123, 111.

[3] *Congressional Record,* 84th Cong., 2nd Sess., D642 ("Daily Digest").

liminary consideration to bills and resolutions. When the number of legislative committee reports became too numerous, other means were necessary for arranging the daily program on the House floor. In the 84th Congress, 2,698 bills and resolutions were favorably reported by the legislative committees. Had the House devoted eight hours to debate, five days each week, for two years, it would have been able to consider each measure for an average of four-and-a-half hours. Actually, during 1955-56, the House met for 937 hours and 16 minutes. Had the time been divided equally among all the measures reported by legislative committees, about twenty minutes could have been given each proposal.

To set the agenda and allocate time for debate on bills that reach the floor, the House has developed a complicated and elaborate set of procedures. Among them are five calendars, three special legislative days, unanimous consent agreements, motions to suspend the *Rules* (which require a two-thirds majority of those voting), and resolutions from the Committee on Rules. These formal procedures are employed chiefly by the Majority Leader and the Speaker after consultation with the Minority Leader, legislative committee chairmen and the "ranking," i.e., senior, committee members among the minority, and the Chairman of the Rules Committee. A comparison of the use of these parliamentary forms to select and dispose of bills and resolutions on the House floor is a good starting point toward a better understanding of the Rules Committee.

THE CALENDARS

When legislative committees approve bills referred to them, the bills are then reported to one of three calendars, which are in fact lists of bills awaiting debate. The Union Calendar contains all proposed money measures, for either revenue or appropriations. The House Calendar is for nonmoney measures. The Private Calendar includes only measures providing specific relief in individual cases. The Consent Calendar consists of requests of members that bills and resolutions on either the Union or House calendars be considered without debate and passed with virtual unanimity.

The Private and Consent calendars are the avenues by which the largest quantity of legislation becomes law. Bills so routed are the least controversial. A private bill is given little notice after it passes the committee stage. Proposals on the Consent Calendar are watched by an Objectors' Committee of three or four members appointed by the floor leader of each party. These members are charged with scrutinizing items on this calendar. On the first and third Mondays of each month, the bills and resolutions on the Consent Calendar are called in their numerical order. A single objection postpones a decision on the bill until the next call, when three objections will strike it from the Consent Calendar for the remainder of the session. If no objections are heard on the first call or fewer than three on the second, the bill passes the House.[4] A bill failing passage on the second call can be considered later under another procedure, e.g., suspension of the rules or a special order from the Rules Committee.

Closely akin to the Private and Consent calendar procedure is suspension of the rules. During the regular order of business the House may, by a two-thirds vote or, more often, by unanimous consent, agree to suspend its rules to consider and pass noncontroversial bills and resolutions. Approximately nine-tenths of the legislation passed in the House at any session is considered under one of these three expeditious procedures, as illustrated by the data in Table 1, which covers eight sessions of Congress.

A less favored method of bringing legislation to the floor is the Discharge Petition and the Discharge Calendar. Under the *Rules* a committee that refuses to report a bill or resolution may be relieved of it upon a motion signed by a simple majority of the House, 218 members.[5] Whenever a Discharge Petition receives the required

---

[4] For a statement of the policies of the Objectors' Committees, see *Congressional Record,* 85th Cong., 1st Sess., p. 2249.

[5] *Rules of the House of Representatives* (Washington: Government Printing Office, 1957), Rule XXVII, clause 4. On the origin and application of the discharge petition, see Floyd M. Riddick, *Congressional Procedure* (Boston: Chapman and Grimes, 1941), pp. 271-300.

Table 1

**PARLIAMENTARY MEANS BY WHICH BILLS AND
RESOLUTIONS PASS THE HOUSE**

CONGRESS-SESSION	Total no. passed	Consent calendar	Private calendar	D. C. day	Rules suspension	Unanimous consent	Special rule
82-1	1,201	150+	588	25-50	12+	100+	48
82-2	1,239	195	568	29	20	328	31
83-1	1,048	201	405	28	7	313	66
83-2	1,600	283	763	32	18	scores	81
84-1	1,597	274	762	25	25	about 100	63
84-2	1,236	337	331	39	52	many	83
85-1	1,198	223	497	34	35	many	57
85-2	1,348	297	469	38	125	many	72
86-1	1,142	265	349	31	52	many	66
86-2	975	211	313	41	53	many	61
87-1	1,234	291	399	39	74	many	49
87-2	1,190	293	424	44	66	many	81

Source: This table is compiled from statistics furnished in Floyd M. Riddick's annual articles on Congress in *Western Political Quarterly* (1952-59). Complete citations are in the bibliography.

number of signatures, the bill or resolution against which it is filed is printed on the Discharge Calendar. On the second and fourth Mondays of each month these measures are taken up in the order in which they have been entered on that calendar.

Only a small percentage of the Discharge Petitions filed commands signatures necessary to reach the Discharge Calendar, as Table 2 reveals.

And, although about one-third of the bills that actually are listed on the Calendar pass the House, only two measures coming to debate via the discharge route have ever been enacted into law. Except for the Wage and Hour Act of 1938 and the Federal Pay Raise Act of 1960, the Senate or the President has always rejected or withheld agreement with the House on bills passed by that body following application of the discharge procedure. The Discharge Petition, then, is in reality little more than a formal guarantee that the majority of the House will not be thwarted in its attempt to express itself on a given issue. As a practical matter it is rarely used and even more rarely successful in enacting legislation.

The House's *internal* norm opposes use of discharge proceedings.

Table 2

USE OF DISCHARGE PETITION AND DISCHARGE CALENDAR TO CONSIDER BILLS

CONGRESS	Number of discharge petitions filed	Number with sufficient signatures to go on calendar	Number passed	Number which became law
75th	43	4	2	1
76th	36	3	2	0
77th	15	1	1	0
78th	21	3	3	0
79th	?	3	1	0
80th	20	1	1	0
81st	34	3	1	0
82nd	14	0	0	0
83rd	10	1	1	0
84th	5	1	0	0
85th	7	1	1	0
86th	7	1	1	1
TOTAL	212+	22	14	2

Source: This table is compiled from data collected and published by Riddick. See *Congressional Procedure* (Boston: Chapman and Grimes, 1941), p. 297, and his annual articles on Congress in the *American Political Science Review* (1939-49) and *Western Political Quarterly* (since 1950).

The action resembles a vote of "no confidence" in a group of colleagues and is also an indirect indictment of the committee system, which is highly esteemed within Congress, whatever outsiders may think of it. Furthermore, members adhere to the golden rule, lest their own committees be discharged. On the other hand, there is an *external* pressure from effective interest groups to sign the petition that would benefit their legislation. On the whole, the internal organizational pressure outweighs the external demands, as evidenced by the small percentage of Discharge Petitions that obtain enough signatures to go on the Discharge Calendar.

SPECIAL LEGISLATIVE DAYS

In addition to the days on which the Consent, Private, and Discharge calendars are called, there are three other special legislative days. These allow consideration of the work from the Committee on the District of Columbia, measures under suspension of the rules, and bills from any committee on Calendar Wednesday.

On the second and fourth Mondays, after matters pending on the Discharge Calendar have been dealt with, the District of Columbia Committee may be recognized to bring up matters within its jurisdiction. Similarly, on the first and third Mondays, following the call of the Consent Calendar, members and committees may be recognized to call up bills under suspension of the rules.[6] A two-thirds vote is required to suspend the rules; the bill must be voted up or down without amendments; and debate is limited to forty minutes. As Table 1 indicates, in recent sessions only a handful of bills have passed under this procedure.[7]

Representatives Sam Rayburn and John McCormack, in opposing the Republican majority's use of suspension of rules proceedings to call up a measure during the 83rd Congress, revealed something of the manner in which the two parties' leaders work within the formal House rules and procedures. Rayburn told the House,

> . . . I do not think while I was either Speaker or Majority Leader that I ever called up, or allowed to be called up under suspension of the rules, any bill until I had consulted with the Minority Leader. If my memory serves me correctly, I never recognized any member to move to suspend the rules unless it was agreeable to the Minority Leader.[8]

And Representative McCormack, at that time Rayburn's second-in-command and Majority Leader when the Democrats organized the

---

[6] Rule XXVII, clause 1.

[7] Near the end of the 85th Congress in 1958, the Democratic leadership put down thirty-five measures on a single suspension Monday, reportedly the largest number ever scheduled under that procedure. Some of these matters were highly controversial, including housing and labor legislation, and because of Rules Committee inaction could not otherwise be considered. A compromise housing bill received a majority vote but failed of passage because it lacked the necessary two-thirds concurrence. The labor bill failed to win even a simple majority. See *Congressional Record*, 85th Cong., 2nd Sess., August 18, 1958.

[8] *Congressional Record*, 83rd Cong., 2nd Sess., p. 11134.

House and Whip when they were in the minority, recalled that:

> Whenever there was a suspension, even on regular Consent Calendar day, when I was Majority Leader, I always advised the minority leadership what was to be put down, and any time they said they did not want this or that bill I respected their wishes.[9]

In short, there is no attempt to deceive the opposition leaders. Instead, the norm is co-operation among leaders of both parties based on mutual consideration and consultation.

The final special legislative day to be mentioned is Calendar Wednesday. Adopted in 1909, it provides for calling the roll of committees every Wednesday.[10] Any committee may then bring up bills that it has previously reported to the House or Union calendars but that have not been considered either in the regular order of business or by special rule. This procedure has not, however, proved to be a practicable means for accomplishing a great amount of business, as Table 3 reveals. Unless there is an understanding among House leaders, very few bills of any importance can be considered in a single Wednesday afternoon session. When Calendar Wednesday is used to bring up bills, it is with an agreement among committee chairmen and the leadership. By previous arrangement with the leadership, occasionally a committee far down the roll will be reached, and one or several bills may be considered.

If this device were resorted to regularly for the consideration of important and controversial matters, the log jam created would be considerable. The rule is that the call of committees shall resume where it stopped at the end of the previous Wednesday. If each committee consumed all the time on one Wednesday, twenty weeks would elapse before all committees would be called. At most, each committee would have two Wednesdays each session. For this reason Calendar Wednesday is often by-passed entirely during a Congress. The leadership, instead, will ask unanimous consent or suspension

---

9 *Ibid.*, p. 11244.
10 Rule XXIV, clauses 4 and 7.

Table 3

USE OF CALENDAR WEDNESDAY TO BRING ISSUES TO THE FLOOR

CONGRESS	Number of Wednesdays on which committees were called	Number of committees called	Number responding	Number of bills and resolutions called up
77th	9	24	9	28
78th	0	0	0	0
79th	4	10	5	6
80th	0	0	0	0
81st	10	14	10	11
82nd	1	19	1	11
83rd	0	0	0	0
84th	1	?	1	1
85th	0	0	0	0
86th	3	5	1	1
87th	1	1	1	1

Source: This table is based on Riddick's annual articles.

of the rules to forego the call of committees. As a result, very few bills are disposed of under this procedure.

As Table 1 has shown, approximately nine-tenths of the bills and resolutions that pass the House are noncontroversial and are adopted after little or no debate. On large numbers of issues the House adopts—virtually without review—the recommendations of its legislative committees, the Committee of Objectors, and the party leaders. The parliamentary forms by which most of the House's decisions are taken are the Consent Calendar, the Private Calendar, and motions for unanimous consent. Several measures pass annually after limited debate on District of Columbia days, but very few bills in recent years have passed on motions to suspend the rules, and still fewer have been enacted following House approval on Calendar Wednesday or after being placed on the Discharge Calendar.

SPECIAL RULES

When an accounting has been made of the essentially noncontroversial work of the House, approximately one hundred bills and resolutions remain each session to occupy the House's attention, and it is on these items that controversy centers. The outcome of elections and the writing of history depend on how the House disposes of these remaining issues. If Congress should fail to pass a private bill admitting an alien to residence or honoring a claim, few people will know and fewer still will care deeply. However much time individual Congressmen or committees or their staffs give to the thousand or so noncontroversial items passed each session, the nation's attentive publics center interest on and judge Congress by its action on the questions relating to labor, agriculture, veterans, health, education, foreign policy, civil rights, welfare, and any other bills that, owing to the times, become contested.

These controversial bills cannot ordinarily be disposed of by the parliamentary measures already discussed. To get them on the agenda of the full House, legislative committee chairmen write a letter to the Committee on Rules requesting a hearing for the purpose of obtaining a "rule" to have the bill considered in the House. If such a rule is reported by the Rules Committee, one of its members would call it up on the floor and, if approved by the House, the legislative committee would then move that the House go into the Committee of the Whole to debate the bill. In other words, then, the Rules Committee participates in making some of the decisions about what bills will be considered in the House, and when.

Participation in making decisions may be taken as a definition of power.[11] To analyze the Rules Committee's power, first consider its power *base,* i.e., the resources and opportunities it has to affect the House's agenda. Most of these resources and opportunities will

[11] The categories for discussing the Committee's power follow Harold D. Lasswell and Abraham Kaplan, *Power and Society* (New Haven: Yale University Press, 1950), pp. 55-102. Also see James A. Robinson, *Congress and Foreign Policy-Making* (Homewood, Ill.: Dorsey Press, 1962), pp. 1-22.

be discussed in greater detail in subsequent chapters; the following paragraphs will review and introduce them.

First, the Rules Committee decides whether to hear a request for a rule. If no hearing is held, i.e., if House members are not given an opportunity to tell the Committee their views about the bill on which a rule is requested, it is unlikely that the Committee will grant a rule. If a hearing is granted, the bill moves one step closer to passage. However, the granting of a hearing in no way insures victory, while refusal of a hearing means a probable defeat.

Second, following a hearing, the Committee decides whether to grant the requested rule. A negative decision increases the probability of defeat for the bill, because if it is so controversial that it cannot win Rules Committee clearance, it is unlikely to pass by suspension of the rules, Calendar Wednesday, or unanimous consent. On the other hand, an affirmative decision merely moves the bill one stage further through the legislative maze. A rule does not assure passage, although no rule most probably assures defeat.

Third, in exchange for a rule, the Committee may require that the bill be modified. When this kind of bargain is struck, the legislative committee usually agrees to offer certain amendments when the bill reaches the floor. Sometimes the Rules Committee will write the rule in such a way as to give preference to a particular amendment or to a substitute bill by requiring that this alternative be voted upon first.

Fourth, the Rules Committee may grant different kinds of rules, and these may have the effect of helping or hindering legislation. Closed rules prohibit amendments; open rules permit them. Rules with stipulated time limits (in number of hours) bring a vote at a predictable time, whereas rules that provide a certain number of days of debate are subject to the whims of quorums and adjournments. Moreover, rules that waive points of order against bills about which there may be some parliamentary question will help the bills.

Fifth, the Rules Committee participates in resolving differences in Senate and House versions of the same bill when any member of the House objects to sending a bill to a conference committee of the two

Houses. In these cases, the Rules Committee may or may not grant a rule to send the bill to conference or to agree to the Senate version. A negative decision by the Committee cannot be reversed, except by the Committee itself, under the pressure of the Speaker, or by the laborious discharge proceedings. An affirmative decision moves the bill much closer to enactment.

Sixth, the Rules Committee has additional power resources near the end of a session of Congress because less time remains for using any of the alternative procedures. Calendar Wednesdays are less frequent; discharge petitions require time for organizing signatures; and the suspension calendar is crowded.

Seventh, when legislative committees compete for jurisdiction of a bill and are in dispute about whether it should go to the House floor and under what conditions, the Rules Committee arbitrates. A negative decision is almost sufficient action to defeat the measure, but an affirmative decision only pushes it to still another stage in the legislative process.

So far, seven opportunities of the Committee for participating in decisions about the House agenda have been listed. All of them are occasions in which the Committee awaits the initiative of some other person or group, a legislative committee chairman, or the House leadership. In none of these instances does—or can—the Committee take the initiative itself. There is, however, an *eighth* opportunity, one that gives the Committee authority to report bills directly to the House floor, whether they have been considered or approved by legislative committees. This base of power is rarely used, however.

If these are the *bases* of the Committee's power, what are its *means* for implementing these resources? First, there is the *actual exercise* of a decision on any of the eight opportunities. Bear in mind that affirmative decisions help but do not assure passage, while negative decisions are difficult to reverse. So it is the actual exercise of a negative decision that is the greatest potential means of power. However, as Chapter 2 will elaborate, actually the Committee makes a relatively small number of negative decisions on both requests for hearings and requests for rules.

As a result, its important means of power are *delay* in granting affirmative decisions and the *threat* of negative decisions. Delay and threat combine to add obstacles to the passage of a bill and sometimes to force changes in it in order to obtain a rule.

Threat has also been used to initiate action, but very infrequently. Only two cases have been publicly known in more than twenty-five years. One was in the 83rd Congress (1953-54) when the Ways and Means Committee refused to report an Eisenhower Administration bill to extend excess profits and excise taxes. The Rules Committee's threat to report a tax bill directly forced the Ways and Means Committee to bring out the measure under its own control.

The case in which the Rules Committee used its power to expedite policies which especially interested it was that of H. R. 3, 85th Congress (1957-58). This bill, introduced by Chairman Howard W. Smith (Democrat, Virginia), declared that no Act of Congress should be interpreted as prohibiting the states to legislate on the same subject unless the act specifically excluded state legislation. The movement for H. R. 3 grew out of more than an abstract protectiveness of Congressional prerogatives from judicial invasion. At that time, certain decisions of the Supreme Court on sedition were genuinely unpopular in the House, and one of these had interpreted the Alien Registration Act of 1940, of which Judge Smith was also author, in a way that many Congressmen, including its author, believed was contrary to legislative intent. What made the issue particularly explosive was that southern opponents of the Court's actions on civil rights were thought to be using the sedition cases as an oblique way of reprimanding the Justices.

Chairman Smith introduced his bill to correct the disputed decisions early in the 85th Congress in 1957. But more than a year later the Committee on Judiciary had not taken favorable action. Then, on March 5, 1958, the Chairman of the Judiciary Committee, Emmanuel Celler (Democrat, New York), appeared before the Rules Committee to request a rule on a relatively minor bill to increase patent fees. During Mr. Celler's ten- or fifteen-minute statement, Judge Smith was seen to motion Clarence Brown (Republican, Ohio) to move up a seat so they could talk.

When Celler completed his testimony, Mr. Brown asked one question about the patent fees and then made an inquiry of a different kind. "Mannie," he prefaced his question, "you don't come up here as often as some of us would like to see you." He would like to take this opportunity, Brown continued, to ask about a bill the Chairman of the Rules Committee had pending before the Judiciary Committee. Judge Smith, Brown said, was too modest to inquire, but Celler ought to be told that there had been discussion in the Rules Committee about reporting H. R. 3 directly to the House floor, a rare and unusual action, but one within the Rules Committee's authority.

Celler said he hoped this would not happen, that no chairman likes to see his committee discharged. He had referred H. R. 3 to a subcommittee and thought it had reported the bill unfavorably. Smith intervened to say that the bill had been reported neither favorably nor unfavorably. Celler said he had asked Judge Smith to appear before the full Judiciary Committee, but had received no response to the invitation.

Brown spoke again to say he did not believe in "horse-trading," but wondered what could be done to expedite H. R. 3. Celler admitted to a liking for "horse-trading," and implied he might hasten action on Smith's bill if the Chairman of the Rules Committee could see his way clear to assist in granting a rule on the so-called premerger notification bill. Smith allowed that "I'm a horse-trader and the son of a horse-trader." When the laughter subsided, Celler asked Smith whether he wanted to meet with the Judiciary Committee, but the Judge declined, saying he just wanted the bill voted up or down.

A few days later Chairman Smith called up a rule but devoted his time not to the pending rule and bill, but to H. R. 3 instead. "I think this discussion may stimulate the thing a little bit in the Judiciary Committee," said Smith. "That was the purpose of it. They are very fine folks over there."

Mr. Celler countered, "What is sauce for the goose is sauce for the gander," and he asked about action on his premerger notification bill.[12]

[12] *Congressional Record,* 85th Cong., 2nd Sess., March 18, 1958.

Within another two months the Judiciary Committee reported H. R. 3. By a 6 to 5 vote the Rules Committee sent it to the floor, where it passed by a large majority, but late in the session the Senate tabled it 41 to 40. The measure obviously had considerable support, but whether it would have reached the floor without Judge Smith's use of his position as Chairman of the Rules Committee is doubtful.

A fourth means of power—in addition to exercise, delay, and threat—is the *anticipation* of one of these. Exercise, delay, and threat are more or less explicit means of action. However, there is a familiar process of "anticipated reaction," in which one party to a situation alters its own action in anticipation of the other party's behavior. In the absence of data from legislative committee executive sessions or interviews throughout the House,[13] it is not possible to verify the presence or the extent of this power mechanism, but members of the Rules Committee assume that it operates. As one member said, "It is the psychological effect. Every committee chairman knows whether the Rules Committee will approve a bill or not. And the chairman will move in the direction of the Rules Committee in trying to get a rule."

These, then, are the eight principal *bases* of power possessed by the Committee on Rules and four *means* or instruments by which these resources may be employed. The *extent* or amount of power that the Committee possesses in the House and through the House in national politics can now be characterized. In doing so, one should specify the *weight, scope,* and *domain* of Committee power.

Weight of power refers to that stage of the policy process in which the Committee participates. The total span of the policy process may be divided into stages of intelligence (problem identification and information gathering), recommendation (alternative formulation), prescription (selection of alternatives), invocation, application, appraisal, and termination. The Rules Committee does not identify problems for Congressional action, nor gather independent information on public questions. As stated previously, it is extraordinary for it to initiate alternatives. Instead, it awaits the initiative of other com-

[13] A current study of the Rules Committee by Professor Robert L. Peabody of The Johns Hopkins University will shed light on this question.

mittees and is not involved in House decision-making until the time comes to set the agenda of the House preparatory to prescribing or selecting a particular course of action. In performing this function of the policy process, the Committee's power and potential power are negative, not innovative. The Committee is a hurdle in the long obstacle course that any bill must successfully complete to become law. The Rules Committee may trip a bill or slow it down or defeat it altogether, but it can do little to propel its passage or assure its success.

To characterize the Rules Committee's power as negative is not to underestimate its importance. Nevertheless, negative power that is available at only certain stages of the policy process should not be overestimated. The power to initiate new programs rests elsewhere in Congress—indeed, elsewhere in the total political system. By and large, the origin of most new policy alternatives is with the executive branch, as is the identification of problems and the collection of information on them. The Rules Committee is just one strategically situated "veto group," in David Riesman's terms, between initiative and decision.

Scope of power refers to the specific issue or substantive content of the policies that are affected. Congress considers a very wide range of policy issues every session, and any scheme for summarizing and classifying them seems oversimplified. But some "shorthand" categories are necessary to reduce the welter of data to manageable terms. The timeworn categories of foreign/domestic and liberal/conservative will serve this purpose.

Holbert N. Carroll, in his extensive work on the House of Representatives and foreign policy-making,[14] reviews twelve years of Rules Committee decisions affecting foreign affairs. He cites a seven-week delay by the Committee in clearing a bill giving India wheat to relieve a grain famine, at the end of which the bill was revised to provide that India borrow money to buy the surplus United States grain rather than receive it as a gift. He recalls other cases, but concludes

[14] *The House of Representatives and Foreign Affairs,* pp. 256-61.

that "there is no evidence to substantiate a conclusion that the rules group is harder on foreign than domestic policies."

The domestic policies that have suffered most at the hands of the Committee are those that pertain to social welfare. In the language of Lasswell and Kaplan,[15] they are "welfare values" as distinguished from "deference values," that is, *well-being, wealth, skill,* and *enlightenment.* Throughout the 1940's and 1950's, the Committee probably refused more rules from the Committee on Education and Labor than from any other committee of the House. Many of its members were especially vigilant in scrutinizing policies of organized labor. Whether the reader agrees with the Committee decisions about labor legislation is not the concern of this book. The fact is that Howard Smith and Eugene Cox (Democrat, Georgia) paid considerable attention to labor policies and from their positions on the Rules Committee affected the legislation on this subject.

As an example, consider the case of the Wage and Hour Act. Among critics of the Rules Committee the most notorious case of Committee "irresponsibility" was its handling of the request for a rule on the Wage and Hour Act in 1937 and 1938. James McGregor Burns has reviewed the circumstances surrounding the Rules Committee's role in the legislative history of that bill.[16] His account lists the Committee as one of the means by which a "minority" nearly defeated a majority. In August, 1937, the Committee declined to grant a rule for the consideration of the bill on the floor. The Committee usually has been blamed for arbitrarily withholding from the House, against the wishes of the majority leadership, a measure that the majority was prepared to enact.

However, Burns also notes that there were not enough Democrats who favored the bill to constitute a quorum for an official party caucus to bind the whole Democratic Congressional contingent. Furthermore, at a special session of Congress in the late fall of 1937, a Discharge Petition against the Rules Committee, after a slow start, received sufficient signatures only after the Administration resorted

[15] *Power and Society,* pp. 55-56.
[16] *Congress on Trial,* pp. 68-82.

to elaborate methods of cajolery. When the bill reached the floor, the "majority" disintegrated, and even proponents of fair labor standards joined the opposition to recommit the bill by a vote of 216 to 198. To say that the Rules Committee was defying the majority will of the House in not granting a rule must be qualified in the light of the difficulties in getting a majority in favor of the principle of the bill and then in reaching agreement on a particular draft of the bill.

In the third session of the 75th Congress, which convened early in 1938, proponents of the bill once more sought to line up a united front. The Rules Committee, says Burns, was "as adamant as ever" in its opposition, but a Discharge Petition passed with considerably greater ease than in the previous session. By this time, the majority was better organized and surer of what it wanted. In such a condition, it had much less difficulty in surpassing the obstacle erected by the Rules Committee.

It is obvious that southerners on the Committee used their tactical position to slow up passage of a bill that they very much opposed. On the other hand, they had some effective debaters' points for their position. They had more than mere obstructionism on their side. The difficulties in securing the first Discharge Petition; the failure of the proponents to find a mutually acceptable bill; the inability of the majority party to hold a caucus to bind its members; the refusal of some members to capitulate before President Roosevelt's requests; the House majority in favor of recommittal—all this is evidence that the Committee, in delaying action and denying a rule, may have been closer to "the will of the House" than is sometimes supposed.

Twenty-five years later, in the 87th Congress (1961-62), in spite of the enlargement of the Committee's membership from twelve to fifteen, practically all the bills not heard or all the rules not granted or all the bills modified in exchange for a rule came from the Education Committee and pertained to federal programs of aid to instruction or school construction. The disagreement in the House about this issue provided an appropriate rationalization for Committee members to deny rules to education bills.

Civil rights legislation—including voting rights bills and the Civil

Rights Commission—have been subject to Rules Committee delay, usually through the Chairman's power to postpone hearings and to insist on the presence of a quorum at meetings considering such issues. But the southern Democrats on the Committee have not been able to defeat civil rights rules because the northern Democrats can usually count on the Republican members of the Committee to join them on this issue.

In discussing the scope of the Committee's power as it concerns liberalism and conservatism, a definition of terms is necessary. Liberalism, as used here, signifies change, and conservatism means maintaining the status quo. Other usages are, of course, available for these terms, and no great store is set by the language or jargon employed. The point to be made is that the Rules Committee's negative influence can more readily be employed in behalf of those who wish to conserve the status quo than it can be used by those who wish to change existing policies. Generally speaking, any stage in the legislative process can be used more effectively to defeat action than to initiate it. If opponents of action can win in the Rules Committee (or any single battle in a subcommittee or full committee, or at the White House), they win the whole legislative contest. On the other hand, proponents cannot gain so much from any single victory; they must win at all stages in order to achieve their ends. It is this kind of reasoning that leads one to the conclusion that the scope of Rules Committee power is conservative and resistant to change.

By *domain of power* is meant the number of persons affected by a decision and the relative importance of the consequences of the decision in terms of the preferred values of those affected. Admittedly it is hard to "operationalize" this aspect of research on power. Robert L. Peabody has suggested, however, that if we think of House decisions in three levels of controversy, the Rules Committee is likely to have most influence over the middle level.[17] The least controversial measures can be passed under unanimous consent, suspension of the

[17] "The Committee on Rules and the House Leadership: Some Consequences of Enlargement," *paper delivered at the 1962 annual meeting of the American Political Science Association,* Washington, D. C.

"Aren't You Big Enough to Have a Key of Your Own?"
—*Herblock in The Washington Post.*

rules, or special legislative days. The most controversial, including those which affect large numbers of peoples in important ways—e.g., tax bills and civil rights proposals—can usually be brought to the floor, albeit with delay, by a determined majority leadership or a determined House majority. It is on the middle level of importance and controversy that the Committee is likely to escape public notice and external pressure.

If one looks at the list of bills not reported in Chapter 2, he will be struck by how many he does not remember or never heard of. Most likely these were measures that commanded the attention of a relatively small number of Congressmen, and for one reason or another the Rules Committee was disinclined to give them favorable treatment.

Summary

The power of the Committee rests in its participation in making decisions affecting the agenda of the House. But its jurisdiction runs to only a small, although important, portion of the House's business; most of the work of the House is scheduled by other persons or roles. The base of the Committee's power consists in its opportunities to give or withhold hearings for rules, to give or withhold rules, to trade a change in the bill for a rule, to permit or forbid amendments and set the length of debate, to take advantage of time constraints near the end of a session, to arbitrate differences between legislative committees, and to initiate action in the absence of legislative committee decisions. Its means of power are the actual exercise of these opportunities, plus the delay, threat, or anticipation of their exercises. The extent of its power is limited by the particular time-point in the legislative process in which it participates; the scope of its power especially applies to domestic welfare policies, to which it shows a preference for the status quo; the domain of its power applies particularly to the middle level of controversial and important legislation before the House.

2

Setting the

Agenda

House agenda, the Rules Committee makes several kinds of decisions affecting the passage or defeat of bills and resolutions. The Committee decides (1) whether to hold a hearing to consider granting a rule to a bill; (2) whether to give a rule if it grants a hearing; (3) when to act as arbiter if legislative committees disagree on the kind of rule they want. This chapter summarizes the Committee's decisions on requests for hearings and requests for rules, and its role as arbiter. With these data we shall see how much and what kinds of discretion the Committee exercises and thus identify more precisely its influence in the House. In addition, we shall consider how the House has evaluated the Committee's performance by accepting or altering its decisions. These data will reveal how closely the Committee reflects the will of the House or how independent of, and therefore influential over, the House it is.

HEARINGS DENIED

Just as the House does not consider all measures presented to it, the Rules Committee takes the position that the requests for rules are too numerous for all to be given a hearing. The late Chairman

Adolph Sabath (Democrat, Illinois), when confronted by the dilemma of too little time and too many demands, once told the House:

> . . . it is impossible for the Rules Committee to schedule hearings on all resolutions referred to it. I suggest now for the information of the House that all members who have introduced resolutions and desire hearings make a formal written request for a hearing. Under the rules of the committee, a hearing cannot be scheduled until an application for the same has been submitted.[1]

Nevertheless, the Chairman (who, it will be seen, decides such questions for the Committee), ordinarily denies a small number of requests for hearings. In the 82nd Congress (1951-52) about twenty requests for hearings were not honored, and approximately the same number were not granted in the 83rd (1953-54). During the 84th Congress (1955-56) only four requests were turned down, but in the 85th (1957-58) and the 86th (1959-60) the number rose to twenty-eight and thirty-one. Thus, about twenty requests each Congress are denied.

The subjects on which the Committee has denied hearings have ranged from air-mail subsidies to weather studies. In the 82nd Congress, nine of the twenty requests that the Rules Committee would not hear were considered on the floor by unanimous consent or suspension of the rules. Therefore, the Committee actually prevented the consideration of eleven measures, not twenty. During the 83rd Congress the Chairman did not schedule hearings on such items as Alaskan statehood, river projects, a gift of surgical equipment to Panama, postal personnel classification, and veterans' pension proposals. The four items that the Committee did not hear in the 84th Congress dealt with acquiring land for a Missouri River dam, fees payable to the Patent Office, appointment of judges, and a Senate bill for the disposal of federal property in the Boulder City area.

[1] *Congressional Record,* 76th Cong., 3rd Sess., p. 2164.

In declining to hear requests for rules on such bills, the Committee unquestionably acts in a way to discourage their passage. It adds its judgment to that of the legislative committees that have studied and approved the measures, and thus contributes to the final output of Congress. Although all bills are important to someone (otherwise they would not be introduced), the few sidetracked bills usually are not bills whose scope and domain rank them among the most important or influential matters before the House of Representatives. In other words, these negative actions by the Committee are rather small contributions to public policy. Moreover, the Alaskan statehood resolution, certainly one of the most important measures ignored by the Committee, could have been brought to the floor during the 83rd Congress as a privileged matter from the Committee on Interior and Insular Affairs, as was done in 1958. Or, had the leadership felt the results worth the effort, it probably could have persuaded the Committee to grant the rule, as it did in 1955.

RULES DENIED

The Rules Committee, in the last several Congresses, has refused to grant rules to an average of slightly more than twelve bills per Congress on which it has held hearings. (This contrasts with the average of more than 125 rules per Congress that it does grant after hearings; see Chapter 1.) Although short titles of bills indicate little about their scope and domain, the subjects of rejected bills are enumerated in Table 4. Issues relating to veterans, public power, reclamation, and conservation seem to be most numerous.

Table 4

SUBJECTS OF BILLS FOR WHICH RULES COMMITTEE WOULD NOT GRANT RULES: 80th TO 86th CONGRESS

80th Congress   Total: 14
Veterans' wages and allowance for job training
To provide annuities for investigatory personnel of FBI
Purchase of automobiles for disabled veterans

Monopolies
Amend Civil Service Retirement Act
Reorganization of debtor railroads
Veterans
Membership in World Health Organization
Temporary embargo on oil
Veterans
Veterans
A national park
To stimulate conservation of strategic minerals
To amend National Housing Act

81st Congress   Total: 35
Rivers and Harbors
Hawaiian statehood
Central Valley Project
Alaskan statehood
Mine Incentives Division in Interior Department
Reclamation and water for irrigation
To increase funds for national forest land survey
Veterans' pension bill
Resident commissioner for Virgin Islands
To extend Economic Co-operation Administration
To authorize the Secretary of Interior to construct, operate and maintain
    Vernigo reclamation project, New Mexico
Extra benefits to civil service annuitants who retired prior to April 1, 1948
Settlement of Alaska by war veterans
National Science Foundation
Encourage exploration for ores, metals, and minerals
Professional health training act
Veterans' hospital
Amend National Housing Act
U. S. participation in international organization
Temporary appropriation
Lodge-Gossett resolution to revise electoral college
To encourage mineral conservation
Railway Labor Act
To amend Reclamation Project Act
Fair Employment Practices Commission
To stimulate exploration for strategic and critical ores and minerals
Budget and Accounting Act
Bankhead-Jones Farm Tenant Act
To increase criminal penalties under Sherman Anti-Trust Act
Temporary extension of import control
Tuna Convention Act
To require certain common carriers to install communications system

To amend Trading with the Enemy Act
Federal Airport Act
To facilitate deportation of aliens

82nd Congress   Total: 8
Construction and maintenance of generating plants in Northwest
Social security and unemployment benefits for federal civilian employees
To prohibit justices and judges of the U. S. from testifying to the
    character and reputation of any person
For relief of certain U. S. employees who, while in the performance of their
    respective duties, suffered losses of personal property by reason of the
    outbreak of hostilities in Korea
Water diversion of Lake Michigan
Jury commission for each district court
Amend Defense Production Act (re: price ceilings)
Instructions to juries in criminal cases

83rd Congress   Total: 8
To send Hawaiian statehood as amended by Senate to include Alaska
    to conference
Quorum of board of National Science Foundation
Chief Joseph Dam
Surface rights and mining claims
To authorize International Joint Commission on United States Canadian
    boundary waters to make a survey of proposed Passamaquoddy tidal
    water power project
Providing that no stamped or other envelope furnished or sold by the Post
    Office Department shall contain any lithographing, engraving, or printing
Federal construction contract act
Independent offices appropriation bill (waiver of points of order)

84th Congress   Total: 11
Washita River Basin reclamation project in Oklahoma
Independent office appropriation bill (waiver of points of order)
To request Secretary of State to carry out certain recommendations of the
    Select Committee on Communist Aggression
To permit and assist federal personnel, including members of the Armed
    Forces and their families, to exercise their voting franchise
Doctors' military draft
Regular and supplemental appropriation
Federal assistance to states
Soil bank
Housing
Niagara power
Section 22 of the Interstate Commerce Act

85th Congress   Total: 9

Effective regulation of the Washington, D. C., Transit System

Amend the Employment Act of 1946 for more effective administration

Comprehensive operation of hydroelectric power resources of the United States

Amend the Legislative Reorganization Act of 1946 re a review of administrative regulations

Omnibus Judgeship Bill

Establish a joint Congressional Commission on Salary Adjustments

Create a joint office on a national fuels policy

Create a select committee to investigate and study the powers and functions of agencies over operation of aircraft

Amend the rules of the House of Representatives (sub-section No. 3 of rule XXII)

86th Congress   Total: 11

Fix fees payable to the Patent Office

Establish a Congressional Award for Scientific Achievement

Revise the status of forces agreements and certain other treaties and international agreements—so that foreign countries will not have criminal jurisdiction over American Armed Forces personnel stationed within their boundaries

Appointment of special joint committee to study and report on the need to extend the capitol

Appoint a committee regarding the conduct of House investigations

Amend the Rules of the House to limit the expenditures for fiscal 1958

Create a committee to conduct an investigation of federal grants-in-aid

Amend Rule XI of the Rules of the House to provide for a study by the House Ways and Means Committee

Study censorship practices of the radio and TV networks (four hearings)

Arkansas Fryingpan Project—in Colorado

A committee should be created to study and investigate all federal grants-in-aid

That proposals from the committees on Veterans Affairs, Public Works, and Interior and Insular Affairs seem to dominate is not because of any peculiar hostility of the Rules Committee to these committees. Much of the legislation emanating from these committees requires appropriations, and the Rules Committee's regular question, "How much will it cost?" probably accounts for the exceptional difficulty these issues have in winning rules.

In 1945, Mrs. Mary Norton (Democrat, New Jersey), chairman

of the Committee on Education and Labor, criticized the Rules Committee for being especially unfair to her committee:

> I say this from my heart—I think the Rules Committee has been most unfair to the Labor Committee. We have applied for many rules and not one for which we applied has been granted. Two rules for which we did not apply were granted gratuitously with substitutions. I have here a long list I could give you of bills reported from the Labor Committee to bring its bills to the floor of the House. The first one to reach the House under my leadership was the wage and hour bill, brought to the floor by petition to discharge the Rules Committee. Some have been brought up by unanimous consent. Then there was a bill that came up on Calendar Wednesday, and another under suspension of rules. Not a bill from our committee has reached the floor under a fair rule granted by this Committee.[2]

A year after Mrs. Norton's criticism, the Committee on Rules granted a rule to the proposal of Representative Francis Case (Republican, South Dakota) on dealing with industrial and labor disputes by drafting striking workmen. Case was able to obtain a rule within forty-eight hours after he introduced his bill and without the Labor Committee's considering it. The haste with which the Rules Committee acted was matched by the decisive vote by which the House passed the rule, 258 to 114.[3] This was one of only two cases in twenty-four years when the Committee reported a rule that a legislative committee had not requested, although infrequent threats to exercise this authority are made. In 1953 the Republican leadership used this technique to pry a tax bill from a reluctant Ways and Means Committee.[4]

There is no question that in failing to grant a right of way for the committee-approved bills (or as with the Case bill, by-passing the

---

[2] *Hearings before the Committee on Rules on H. R. 2232, 79th Congress, First Session* (Washington: Government Printing Office, 1945), p. 25.

[3] For debate and vote on the rule making the Case bill (H. R. 5262) in order as a substitute for H. R. 4908 (a Labor Committee-sponsored measure), see *Congressional Record*, 79th Cong., 2nd Sess., pp. 661-69.

[4] 83rd Congress, H. Res. 306 for consideration of H. R. 5899, Excess Profits Tax Extension Act.

legislative committee altogether), the Committee on Rules acts as a policy-making as well as a procedural committee. Further, the timing of a bill may contribute to its success or failure on the floor, and as the next chapter will note, the difference between opening or closing a bill to amendment may determine the final form in which it passes. No committee charged with the authority to arrange the consideration of the work of other committees is likely to escape affecting substance. There are degrees of policy-affecting, and in denying a rule to a legislative report, the Rules Committee is more frankly policy-oriented than it is in merely regulating time for debate and freedom of amendment.

ARBITRATION OF COMMITTEE CONFLICTS

The Committee contributes to the formation of public policy in ways other than deciding what to report and when. It has, for example, occasionally acted as broker or arbiter between individuals or even committees in dispute over the content of a rule. The Rules Committee, in such cases, has secured assurances that the legislative committee with original jurisdiction will be prepared to offer corrective amendments on the floor. Or, conversely, it has sought and obtained commitments that the legislative committee will not attempt to alter a bill on the floor.

An example occurred in 1941, when the Committee was asked to clear a defense housing bill. Judging from Chairman Sabath's speech on behalf of the rule, the Committee anticipated objections that might arise on the floor and mediated adjustments in advance.

I am pleased to state that due to the aid and assistance of gentlemen on the left, the committee has reported the rule, and that very little time will be used either on the rule or the bill, because an agreement has been reached, whereby some of the objectionable features have been eliminated. The Rules Committee spent about 6 or 8 days before reporting the rule. They did not wish to do anything that would be displeasing to the committee that reported the bill; but to enable the

Rules Committee to report the bill, we were obliged to obtain a great deal of information that was sought by nearly every member of the Committee on Rules.

. . . I feel that some may regard the work of the Committee on Rules as an encroachment on the prerogatives or legislative function of the Committee on Public Buildings and Grounds, but the members of my committee felt it necessary, as I have stated, to obtain all information on the best possible housing, on its economic construction, and at the same time, to receive assurances that sufficient rentals would be obtained from those who are to have the benefit of these facilities.[5]

On another occasion Sabath announced that the Committee had negotiated an agreement with the Banking and Currency Committee for the amendment of certain provisions in a price control bill.

The Committee on Rules has been informed by several members that there is some opposition to the bill because of certain provisions in section 2 of the bill. I am pleased to report that the chairman of the Committee on Banking and Currency and those members who were present with him at our meeting yesterday assured the Committee on Rules that they will move to strike the verbiage to which some of the members of the [Rules] Committee objected.[6]

In presenting the selective service extension bill to the House in 1945, Eugene Cox (Democrat, Georgia) strongly urged amendments to meet the Rules Committee criticisms.

The reporting of this bill, however, is not to be taken as an indication that all members of the Committee on Rules are enthusiastic about it as written. I think it fails and fails woefully to satisfy the demands of public opinion. The public is looking to the Congress for a work-or-fight bill, and this is no such measure.[7]

Once, in explaining the delay in reporting a rule, Judge Sabath revealed something of the bargaining that can occur between the

[5] *Congressional Record*, 77th Cong., 1st Sess., pp. 2244-45.
[6] *Ibid.*, 77th Cong., 2nd Sess., p. 7260.
[7] *Ibid.*, 79th Cong., 1st Sess., p. 557.

Rules Committee and a legislative committee. ". . . The delay," said Sabath, "in granting the rule was due to the fact that some members of the Committee on Rules feared that the Committee on Banking and Currency might offer amendments with which some of the members did not agree."[8] The Rules Committee, in exchange for a rule, required the Banking and Currency Committee to alter its bill, and then the Rules Committee exacted further assurances that the stricken features would not be offered as amendments when the bill reached the floor.

In 1958 the Banking Committee could not obtain rules for several of its bills until it agreed to offer amendments on the floor to change the method of financing certain depressed area and small business ventures. These projects, like many other federal programs in recent years, were to be paid for by direct borrowing from the Treasury rather than by appropriations approved by the two Congressional committees on appropriations and passed by both Houses. Members of the House Appropriations Committee protested this by-passing of the appropriations process, and the Rules Committee laid down an informal policy that it would grant rules for no new spending programs that borrowed directly from the Treasury although it would do so to continue existing programs. In this case more was at stake than Congressional oversight of federal expenditures; the size of these programs was also at issue. It was commonly assumed that the Appropriations Committee would not report as much money as the legislation authorized. The committees sponsoring the legislation regretted this limitation on their discretion, but they recognized that they could secure no legislation without making these concessions to the alliance between the Rules and Appropriations Committees.[9]

[8] *Ibid.*, 79th Cong., 2nd Sess., p. 1652.

[9] See *Congressional Record*, 85th Cong., 2nd Sess., August 1 and August 15, 1958, and the *New York Times*, August 16, 1958, p. 1, col. 1. For notice that these concessions should not "be taken as a precedent by those who would deny the long-recognized jurisdiction of the legislative committees of both Houses to include provisions for public debt transactions in bills they report," see the Statement by the Managers on the Part of the House appended to the Conference Report (H. Rept. No. 2492) on S. 3651, *Congressional Record*, 85th Cong., 2nd Sess., August 6, 1958.

Such practices on the part of the Rules Committee are not routine, yet the fact remains that, on occasion, by this means the Committee has printed its particular stamp of policy on the bills that it has cleared for floor consideration.

HOUSE REVIEW OF RULES COMMITTEE DECISIONS

The House's evaluation of the decisions of the Rules Committee is expressed in two ways: by its use of procedures to consider bills the Rules Committee will not clear and by its acceptance or rejection of bills the Committee brings to the floor. The first is the House's review of the Committee's negative decisions; the latter, of its affirmative decisions. Frequent reversals of either kind of decision would indicate conflict between the Committee and the House; infrequent reversals may be assumed to indicate accurate representation of the membership.

To reverse negative decisions by the Rules Committee or any other committee, the House may invoke discharge proceedings. Between 1937 and 1958 more than two hundred Discharge Petitions were filed, but only twenty-one (an average of one a session) obtained the requisite number of signatures to be placed on the Discharge Calendar. Thirteen of these passed the House, but only one (the Wage and Hour Act of 1938) also received both Senatorial and Presidential support, thus becoming law. (In 1960 the Federal Pay Raise Act was discharged in the House and eventually enacted.) The record on discharges reveals that the Committee occasionally, but not frequently, fails to schedule a bill that the House favors so strongly that it will take extraordinary measures to by-pass the Committee. Owing to certain norms surrounding the use of discharge proceedings, one might confidently predict that there have been a few other measures that a majority might have supported, if they had reached the floor under normal procedures. However, as noted earlier, there is an understandable reluctance on the part of many members to sign Discharge Petitions. To sign, one must feel rather intensely about the issue; mere passive support probably will not move many members to sign, for one day they and their committees might be the victim of a similar discharge, if the use of this device became a habit.

Further indications of the House's evaluation of the Rules Committee occurred in 1949, 1950, and 1951, when the "21-Day Rule" was initiated, reaffirmed, and finally rescinded (see Chapter 4). This rule permitted the chairmen of the legislative committees to be recognized by the Speaker on two days each month for the purpose of calling up bills on which the Rules Committee had not acted within three weeks after the request for a rule. The 21-Day Rule was initially favored by the Democratic leadership and supporters of President Truman's Fair Deal program (including some Republican Representatives). Opposition consisted largely of the Republican leadership and rank and file, plus southern Democrats. An attempt to repeal the rule was defeated early in 1950, but Republican gains in the Congressional elections of that year were sufficient to permit opponents of the rule to abolish it at the beginning of the 82nd Congress in 1951.

During the one Congress in which by-passing the Rules Committee was rather easier, eight bills that the Committee refused to report reached the floor; seven of them passed. The successful bills concerned rivers and harbors and flood control, statehood for Alaska, statehood for Hawaii, the establishment of the National Science Foundation, an anti-poll tax bill, establishment of a veterans' hospital, and a joint resolution on United States participation in international organizations. Some observers thought a few other bills probably were granted rules on the assumption that they could or would reach the floor under the 21-Day Rule, although the Committee denied more rules during this Congress than in any other on which detailed data are available. The House majority evidently believed that the Committee was out of step with it, but the original majority soon diminished to minority status, and the Committee regained its former prerogatives.

Another instance in which the Committee was by-passed also

occurred in the 81st Congress. A majority of the Committee would not grant the usual resolution providing for immediate consideration of a Senate amendment to the Railway Labor Act. Under an obscure and seldom-used rule allowing for disposal of bills directly from the Speaker's table, the House proceeded to consider and pass the bill.[10]

Thus, parliamentary procedures for reversing negative Committee decisions are not easily implemented, although the House almost annually discharges the Committee once or otherwise considers a bill it would have denied a rule. However, the House's opportunities for accepting, amending, or rejecting the Committee's affirmative decisions are more numerous and more easily invoked.

Once the Rules Committee has reported a rule, the decision to call it up is largely left to the leadership, particularly the Majority Floor Leader, who more than any other person is occupied with determining the agenda of the House. As Chairman John J. O'Connor (Democrat, New York) told the House in 1937, "the Rules Committee never calls up a rule without first consulting with the Speaker and the Majority Floor Leader."[11] Each Saturday the leadership prepares and distributes notices, over the signature of the Whip, setting forth the expected daily program; and near the end of each week the Majority Leader, in response to an inquiry from the Minority Leader, informs the House of the next week's program. Advance announcement of the agenda is a rather recent innovation in House procedure. As late as 1920, complaints were voiced on the floor by minority leaders and many of the majority party that they did not know when the leadership would bring up important matters.[12]

When the leadership decides that a rule from the Committee will be taken up, it seeks out the Committee member who will handle the resolution on the floor. At the appropriate point in the proceedings, that member rises, and upon securing recognition from the

[10] Floyd M. Riddick, "The Eighty-First Congress: First and Second Sessions," *Western Political Quarterly*, 4 (1951), 59.

[11] *Congressional Record*, 75th Cong., 1st Sess., p. 5307.

[12] Robert Luce, *Legislative Procedure* (Boston: Houghton Mifflin Company, 1922), pp. 201-02.

Speaker, makes a statement somewhat as follows: "Mr. Speaker, by direction of the Committee on Rules, I call up House Resolution X and ask for its immediate consideration." Under the *Rules* of the House he is granted one hour's time, half of which by custom he yields to a minority member of the Committee. Ordinarily, any debate on this resolution, like almost all the testimony before the Committee, relates to the substance of the bill for whose consideration the resolution provides, and not to the rule itself.

As Representative Hamilton Fish (Republican, New York) once stated, "Mr. Speaker, as far as I know, there is no opposition to this rule. Therefore, the time under the rule will be used to discuss the bill."[13]

Frequently, the whole hour is not consumed. Of the debates on the rules brought up in the second session of the 82nd Congress, approximately one-half were debated less than five minutes before the previous question was moved. In the second session of the 83rd Congress, forty-four of the ninety-three Rules Committee resolutions acted on by the House were considered for less than a page and a half of the *Congressional Record*. Practice remained the same in the second session of the 84th Congress, when forty-one of the eighty-one rules were debated for less than a page of the *Record* and only about fifteen consumed more than three pages.[14]

In addition to the length of debate as an index of the controversy of the rule, the kind of vote—whether voice, division, or roll call— provides a measure of the opinion of the House. When there is little controversy, measures are passed by voice vote in order to save time. Mildly controversial bills may require a division, i.e., standing, vote. On controversial questions (and on some required in the Constitution), the roll is called and each member answers individually. Christopher Van Hollen counted 94 roll calls on rules between 1933 and 1951 and computed that these amounted to only 14 per cent of

---

[13] *Congressional Record,* 77th Cong., 1st Sess., p. 8763.
[14] Floyd M. Riddick, "The Eighty-Second Congress: Second Session," *Western Political Quarterly,* 5 (1952), 626, n. 34; "The Eighty-Third Congress: Second Session," *ibid.,* 7 (1954), 647; "The Eighty-Fourth Congress: Second Session," *ibid.,* 10 (1957), 71.

the total number of rules considered by the House.[15] And as Riddick observes, some of these may be required because a quorum is not present,[16] not because of the controversial character of the rule. The evidence is that most rules are not the subject of controversy.

Of the controversial rules, the House rejects very few. In the twenty-four years from 1937 to 1960 only twenty-four rules were defeated (see Table 5). With two exceptions, they were voted down not because the House thought the rules unfair or inadequate, but because it was opposed to the bills that they would have brought to the floor. Representative J. Will Taylor (Republican, Tennessee) summarized the general practice while announcing his own position: ". . . I am opposed to this rule and voted against it in the Rules Committee because I am opposed to the resolution which it harbingers."[17]

Of the two exceptions to this generalization, one has been cited as an example of Rules Committee usurpation of the prerogatives of other committees.[18] In 1944 a delegation from the Committee on Banking and Currency appeared before the Rules Committee to request clearance for H. R. 4941, to extend the Emergency Price Control Act of 1942. During the same year Representative Howard W. Smith (Democrat, Virginia), a member of the Rules Committee, had secured a resolution from that committee, which the House adopted, to create a special committee to investigate the Office of Price Administration. Smith was made chairman of the investigating committee. As Representative John J. Cochran (Democrat, Missouri) said on the floor of the House, "No one can deny but that the gentleman from Virginia is a powerful member of the Rules Committee."[19] In addition to investigating the OPA, Smith's twenty-one-man special committee filed a report proposing legislation to alleviate

---

[15] *The House Committee on Rules (1933-1951): Agent of Party and Agent of Opposition* (Ph.D. dissertation, The Johns Hopkins University, 1951), p. 67.

[16] "The Eighty-Second Congress: Second Session," p. 647.

[17] *Congressional Record*, 76th Cong., 1st Sess., p. 4408.

[18] Roland Young, *Congressional Politics in the Second World War* (New York: Columbia University Press, 1956), pp. 115-16.

[19] *Congressional Record*, 78th Cong., 2nd Sess., p. 5470.

Table 5

BILLS FOR WHOSE CONSIDERATION RULES WERE DEFEATED

75th Congress
H. Res. 526 (H. J. Res. 671) Bureau of Fine Arts (Open: 1 hour)
H. Res. 522 (S. 2838) Camp Springs, Md., Airport (Open: 1 hour)

76th Congress
H. Res. 286 (H. R. 7120) RFC projects (Open: 5 hours)
H. Res. 266 (S. 591) Public Housing (Open: 4 hours)
H. Res. 406 (H. R. 3157) Homesteads (Open: 4 hours)

77th Congress
None

78th Congress
H. Res. 582 (H. R. 4941) Price Control (Open: 9 hours, Smith bill in order
    as amendments)
H. Res. 593 (H. R. 4901) To sell Moore, Oklahoma Air Field (Open: 2 hours)

79th Congress
H. Res. 248 (H. R. 1270) Carden-Herd claims appeal (Open: 1 hour)
H. Res. 407 (H. R. 3937) Repeal War Labor Act (Open: 2 hours)
H. Res. 452 (H. R. 4199) Retirement for elected officials (Open: 2 hours)

80th Congress
None

81st Congress
H. Res. 842 (H. R. 8920) Re: action on Senate Amendments to tax revision
H. Res. 716 (H. R. 6277) Re: Russian Railway Service (Open: 1 hour)
H. Res. 818 (S. 784) Relief of steamship companies (Open: 1 hour)

82nd Congress
H. Res. 166 (H. R. 2988) Defense housing (Open: 4 hours)
H. Res. 430 (H. R. 82) Irish Unity (Open: 1 hour)
H. Res. 695 (H. R. 7888) To create Joint Committee on Budget (Open:
    2 hours)

83rd Congress
H. Res. 626 (H. R. 236) Fryingpan-Arkansas Project (Open: 2 hours)

84th Congress
H. Res. 312 (H. R. 5222) Amend Flammable Fabrics Act (Open: 1 hour)
H. Res. 641 (H. R. 412) Fryingpan-Arkansas Project (Open: 2 hours)

85th Congress
H. Res. 362 (H. R. 7244) To permit deductions for self-help meat promotion
    program (Open: 1 hour)
H. Res. 485 (H. R. 4504) For handling perishable agricultural commodities
    (Open: 2 hours)

H. Res. 609 (H. R. 12954) Acreage allotments and price supports on certain products (Open: 5 hours—with points of order waived)
H. Res. 650 (S. 3497) Community Facilities Administration loan (Open: 3 hours)

86th Congress
H. Res. 488 (H. R. 2331) To establish Chesapeake and Ohio Canal Historical Park and to maintain a parkway (Open: 2 hours)

alleged grievances in price control administration. Five members dissented and submitted a minority report. The Banking and Currency Committee considered but rejected Smith's proposals.

When the Rules Committee considered a rule for price control extension, Smith moved that the report of his special committee be made in order as a substitute. This was too much to ask even of an independent Rules Committee, for, as Representative Fish observed, such a rule "would have given the right-of-way to the Smith bill over the bill reported by the Committee on Banking and Currency, and the Smith bill would have been considered first and would have had legislative priority."[20] The Rules Committee did, however, agree to an open rule for the price control bill, and included the following provision: "It shall be in order to consider without the intervention of any point of order any amendment which may be offered to the bill embodying any of the sections or paragraphs contained in the bill H. R. 4647." The effect of this provision was to make the Smith bill in order in the form of amendments. The waiver was necessary because parts of the Smith proposal were not germane to the price control extension legislation.

Just before the Chairman of the Rules Committee was scheduled to call up the rule, Judge Smith gained the floor for one hour on a point of personal privilege. Smith, who is acknowledged by friend and foe alike as one of the ablest parliamentarians in the recent history of the House, called attention to an article by a columnist, Marquis Childs. This article, Smith asserted and the Speaker agreed, constituted a personal attack on Smith. Smith used as much of the hour as he could—interspersed by frequent admonitions from the

[20] *Ibid.*, p. 5468.

chair not to go beyond the purpose for which he had gained the floor—to justify his investigation and explain why his report should be in order under the rule soon to be offered. Smith's major contention, aside from attacks on the OPA, was that the House had authorized the investigation, expended $50,000 for it, and was entitled now to pass judgment upon the results of the study.

When Chairman Sabath was recognized, he called up the rule, but spoke in opposition to the Smith proviso. Toward the end of the hour allotted for debate, Speaker Rayburn stepped down from the rostrum and made a four-minute speech opposing the rule. His short remarks deserve notice.

> I ask the pardon of the House for taking the floor at this time, but after 31 years of service in the House of Representatives I am very jealous of the rights, prerogatives, and privileges of the House of Representatives. I am also very jealous of the rights, prerogatives, and privileges of all the committees of the House. . . .
>
> We have before us a bill which the Committee on Banking and Currency patriotically and sensibly considered for a time. They did their work. In the usual way they appeared before the Committee on Rules for a rule for the consideration of their bill. During the consideration, other matters were brought into the committee. I take this time to warn the members of this House, every one of whom is a member of a legislative committee, except those who are members of the Rules Committee and no other committee, the Committee on Rules was never set up to be a legislative committee. It is a committee on procedure, to make it possible that the majority of the House of Representatives may have the opportunity to work its will. If this is orderly, if that part of the rule that is in controversy here is orderly, then the legislative committees of the House might well take care, because the Committee on Rules, under this system, can meet, you can introduce a bill today, refer it to a legislative committee, and the Committee on Rules tomorrow can bring in a rule making it in order. . . .[21]

The Speaker's views triumphed and the rule was defeated, 170 to 44. More precisely, the previous question was defeated. Chairman Brent Spence (Democrat, Kentucky) then offered an amendment to the

[21] *Ibid.*, p. 5471.

rule, which was designed to eliminate the waiver of points of order against the Smith bill. This was adopted, and the Banking and Currency bill was then considered under an open rule for nine hours of debate.

The other occasion during this twenty-year period when the Rules Committee reported a rule that the House amended was in 1950. In September of that year, three months after the outbreak of fighting in Korea, the Committee brought in a rule to take a tax revision bill from the Speaker's table, disagree to the Senate amendments, and send it to conference.[22] As amended in the Senate, the bill contained no tax on excess profits, and certain groups in the House succeeded in defeating the rule, 226 to 105, with the hope of incorporating such a tax in the act before it went to conference. After the previous question had been voted down, Representative Herman P. Eberharter (Democrat, Pennsylvania) offered an amendment to the rule, providing that the measure going to conference include an excess profits tax. Thereupon Representative Wilbur Mills (Democrat, Arkansas) made a point of order, which Speaker Rayburn sustained, that the amendment was not germane. The most Eberharter and his colleagues could achieve was a directive that the Ways and Means Committee study the subject of excess profits, something the Committee already had planned to undertake. When the amended rule was finally adopted and the bill sent to conference, there was little to distinguish the House's action from what would have been the outcome had it passed the rule that the Rules Committee proposed. The defeat of the original rule was scarcely a defeat, inasmuch as the victors failed in their main objective by virtue of their motion's being out of order.

Summary

The Committee grants all but about twenty requests for hearings each Congress. It withholds rules from about twelve bills on which it holds hearings, while giving rules to more than a hundred. It occasionally, but less frequently, arbitrates differences between legis-

---

[22] H. Res. 842 for the consideration of H. R. 8920.

lative committees or intra-committee differences over whether and how a rule should be written. To consider the measures the Committee has refused to report, the House discharges the Committee approximately once a session, and for one Congress it amended its *Rules* to provide for legislative committee chairmen and the leadership to by-pass the Committee after twenty-one days. Of the rules reported, the House averages approximately one defeat each session, but most rules are not controversial enough to require a roll-call vote.

3

Regulating Debate and Allocating Time

Committee on Rules recommend when certain important bills and
resolutions will reach the floor, but it also recommends, subject to
acceptance by a House majority, the rules under which these measures
will be considered. These rules cover the conditions under which the
legislation will be debated and the length of time for debate. Debate
is regulated by one of four kinds of rules. A "closed rule" limits or
prohibits amendments from the floor. An "open rule" allows a bill
to be amended by the House. A third type of rule waives points of
order against all or part of a bill. Finally, a rule may provide for disposing of differences when House and Senate disagree on the language
of an act. The length of debate may be as little as a half-hour or as
much as several days, although in practice one to four hours is the
usual period for argument. This chapter considers both the frequency
with which various types of rules are used and the typical patterns in
allocating the House's time.

CLOSED AND OPEN RULES

The two most frequently used rules are closed and open rules.
Closed rules limit the opportunity of the House to amend the bill
as reported by the legislative committee. The rule may allow no

amendments, certain amendments, or only those offered by the committee with original jurisdiction. The major effect of a closed rule is that the House agrees to limit or forbid itself from altering the committee version of a bill. An open rule allows the bill to be read for amendment under the "five-minute rule," a procedure which affords any member of the House an opportunity to propose an amendment and to speak on it for five minutes. Frequently the five-minute rule is utilized not to amend but to extend the debate that has expired on the bill itself. In this case members introduce *pro forma* amendments "to strike out the last word," speak for five minutes, and sometimes hear five minutes' debate against the amendment, fully expecting the amendments to be defeated automatically.

The closed rule is used much less frequently than the open. In eleven Congresses between 1939 and 1960, the House adopted eighty-seven closed rules and 1,128 open rules. Closed rules are reserved for revenue measures and occasional other complex issues. The leadership uses this device to save such bills from "crippling amendments" (crippling from its point of view). Nearly one-third of the closed rules governed fiscal matters, either taxation or appropriation items. Bills on tariffs, the simplification of customs, and social security typically carry closed rules. A few labor and housing issues and an occasional road or defense bill virtually exhaust the list. Most of these issues are especially allergic to local and regional vote trading, less elegantly known as logrolling. Tariff and tax bills are notorious objects of bargaining among representatives of local and constituent interests, and many amendments, with no apparent relation to any conception of the "national interest," doubtless would be proposed if open rules prevailed. Closed rules confine this kind of bargaining to the committee stage and require the House to accept or reject the committee version as a whole.

Although a practice of both parties, closed rules are almost invariably protested. Cries of "Gag" are heard on the floor from leaders of the minority (who would bring in similar rules were they the majority), as well as from individual members. The majority side of the Rules Committee usually apologizes for—and explains at length—the necessity of a closed rule. For example, read the words of Eugene Cox (Democrat, Georgia) in speaking on behalf of a closed rule for the consideration of a tax bill:

> I should like to make the observation that the Committee reporting this rule would regret that any members of the House should feel that any right is being denied them. Nobody likes this kind of rule. The Committee reporting it does not like to report closed rules. The Committee on Ways and Means, requesting the rule, I know with great reluctance, came to the conclusion that it should ask for this kind of rule. However, common sense, Mr. Speaker, impelled us to the conclusion that it was the only sensible way of considering the bill. This rule preserves the integrity of the measure, which is exceedingly technical and complicated. . . .[1]

The widespread and accepted view of the closed rule with respect to tax bills was expressed by Representative Howard W. Smith (Democrat, Virginia) when opposing a closed rule on an unemployment compensation bill. ". . . We necessarily have to have them on matters pertaining to the revenue act, that is, tax measures. We have them for the reason that it is impossible to write a tax bill on the floor. . . ."[2]

In spite of the usual criticism of "gag rules," none of the twenty-four rules defeated by the House in the two decades between 1937 and 1960 was a closed rule.[3] In 1955 the Reciprocal Trade Agreements renewal act came within five votes of being denied a closed rule, the nearest thing to a defeat ever encountered by any such rule up to this time. Members on both sides of the aisle are resigned to the fact that to open certain subjects to amendment would be to invite unfortunate results for all concerned. In adopting closed rules the majority of the House displays what might be called majority-self-control. So long as the leadership uses the closed rule sparingly

---

[1] *Congressional Record*, 76th Cong., 3d Sess., p. 11233.
[2] *Ibid.*, 83rd Cong., 2nd Sess., p. 10063.
[3] See Table 5 in Chapter 2 (pp. 38-39).

and after consultation with the minority party's leaders, the House is not likely to rebel, however many of its members protest as individuals.

Of the legislative business arranged by the Rules Committee, the bulk is brought to the floor under open rules, which allow the House to amend the committee versions under the five-minute rule. Sometimes the Committee will add to the plain open rule a waiver that allows for the consideration of a particular amendment or an alternative prepared by the committee with original jurisdiction. This practice does not contradict the principle of the open rule, but rather supplements it with an additional alternative for the consideration of the House. Such amendments are frequently the product of a sharply divided committee. Often when the legislative committee and the Rules Committee recognize that a significant number of House members favors the minority report of the legislative committee, or when the minority party's leadership offers a widely supported substitute, the rule will allow for consideration of the alternative.

The difference between what is debated under open and closed rules is not necessarily a difference in importance or even in the intensity of controversy. For example, legislation concerning compulsory military training, lend-lease, the GI Bill of Rights, full employment, foreign aid, minimum wage, civil rights, school construction, and natural gas, all of which would surely rank high in any evaluation of controversial or important policies, has been open to amendment. However, a larger proportion of closed rules than of open rules will be controversial.

In brief, most proposals come up under an open rule, except for those classes of legislation, e.g., tax and appropriation bills, that have a history of being saved from "special interest" amendments. Temporary issues such as price control, which most Congressmen detest and for which there is no tradition of protection against private members' amendments, are likely to receive open rules along with the vast majority of bills, controversial and noncontroversial, processed by the Committee.

WAIVERS OF POINTS OF ORDER

Another type of rule is that which waives points of order against nonprivileged matter in an otherwise privileged measure. Reports from the Committee on Appropriations, for example, lose their privileged status when they contain legislative provisions. The practice has regularly been that the Appropriations Committee goes to the Rules Committee and secures a rule to waive points of order against nonprivileged parts of its bills. Because of their privileged nature, it is unusual for appropriations bills to be considered under a rule, but waivers of points of order or limitations on amendments frequently are obtained by unanimous consent or by a rule from the Committee on Rules.

In the period 1939 to 1956 the Committee on Rules reported and the House adopted forty-seven resolutions to waive points of order against appropriations measures; in the years 1957-60, eighteen waivers were reported for appropriations bills. These included supplemental or deficiency appropriations and moneys for a variety of departments and agencies. There are occasional protests from some members when the Appropriations Committee is permitted to by-pass the *Rules of the House,* although no rule for a waiver of points of order was defeated in the twenty-four year period from 1937 to 1960.[4] Chairman Sabath once warned the House committees that his Committee would not continue to grant waivers against points of order. On the occasion of reporting a rule waiving objections to the inclusion of a legislative provision for the National Youth Administration in a Labor Department appropriation, Sabath said,

Mr. Speaker, the Rules Committee does not look with a great deal of favor on committees bringing in bills, especially calling for appropriations where no authority has been heretofore granted. Not only does the Rules Committee look with disfavor upon the granting of rules of that kind, but the Rules Committee also feels—and I might as

[4] *Ibid.*

well be candid with the House—that henceforth any and all committees that come in for a rule will have to show a clean bill. What I mean is, not come before the Rules Committee and say, "We will amend the bill when it reaches the floor if a rule is granted." The Committee feels that such rules should not be granted and will not be granted in the future. But in this instance we felt that it was for national defense and that the committee having charge of this appropriation bill had carefully examined the need of each and every provision of the bill.[5]

In spite of this promise to get tough with the Appropriations Committee, the Rules Committee continued to report rules waiving points of order in money bills. Two Congresses later, objections to this practice were heard again. For example, Representative John Taber (New York), a leading Republican spokesman on appropriations matters, objected to the inclusion of legislation for a Farm Security Administration and a school lunch program in an appropriations item. He told the House,

I do not think any legislation should be reported in appropriations bills except on emergency matters that relate to national defense. Regulation items should never be brought in. When you have an emergency matter that relates to the national defense it is fair to consider such items matters of expediency and meriting a rule. When you come to regular routine things we should not take them up unless the legislative committees have brought in here and the Congress has authorized appropriations. That is the only way that we can protect the jurisdiction of the various legislative committees.[6]

A few days later Mr. Taber expressed his disapproval of including legislation in appropriations, and Chairman Sabath brought in a rule waiving points of order against appropriations for war agencies. The Chairman took great pains to apologize to the House for this regrettable procedure and complained that ". . . for over four years the Committee on Rules has requested and urged the Committee on Appropriations not to bring in legislation or appropriations bills

[5] *Congressional Record,* 77th Cong., 1st Sess., 1941, p. 4701.
[6] *Ibid.,* 79th Cong., 1st Sess., 1945, p. 2668.

depriving the legislative committee of their functions. . . ."[7] Members argued against this rule because it allowed for the continuation of some war agencies, but not others (notably OPA and FEPC). But, after the usual protestations, the rule was adopted by a voice vote.

Ordinarily, when the Rules Committee hears a request from the Appropriations Committee for a waiver, it also hears members of other committees who may have jurisdiction over the legislative provisions contained in the appropriation. For example, in the 83rd Congress, Representative Harris Ellsworth (Republican, Oregon), in reporting a rule waiving points of order against an appropriation for the Department of Agriculture, assured the House that representatives of the Committee on Agriculture had appeared before the Rules Committee and had no objection to the waiver.[8]

A sharp controversy occurred in the 84th Congress when the Rules Committee declined to grant the Appropriations Committee a rule waiving points of order against one of its bills. The appropriations measure contained legislative provisions that destroyed its privileged character and made it subject to a point of order on the floor. As usual, the committee sought a rule to waive the points of order, but the Rules Committee thought the number of objectionable provisions was unusually high (there were more than thirty) and understood that some of the legislative committees concerned were opposed to certain legislative provisions in the bill.[9] After hearing representatives of the Appropriations Committee, the Rules Committee adjourned without acting decisively on the request for a rule.

Rather than waiting for a possible favorable decision in the Rules Committee, the Appropriations Committee, probably with the concurrence of the leadership, brought in the bill and allowed members to make their objections, thus preventing the House from voting on the questionable provisions. The Rules Committee then came in for caustic criticism from members of the Appropriations Committee.

---

[7] *Ibid.,* p. 5796.

[8] *Ibid.,* 83rd Cong., 2nd Sess., 1954, p. 5000.

[9] See the remarks of Chairman Smith, *Ibid.,* 84th Cong., 1st Sess., 1955, p. 10944.

Chairman Clarence Cannon (Democrat, Missouri), with several decades of experience as parliamentarian, historian, and member of the House, thought that ". . . we have traveled far afield in the interpretation of the functions of the Committee on Rules. . . ." His recollection of the Congressional debates of 1880 and 1911 is the standard one taken by critics of the Rules Committee.

> If you will read the debates on those two revisions with relation to the duties of the Committee on Rules you will find that Committee was not intended to retard legislation. Whenever there was conflict as to priority the Committee on Rules was designed to resolve the conflict. They were to make possible the consideration of a bill which otherwise could not be considered. They were not authorized, it was never intended that they should deny the House the right to pass upon any proposition reported by other committees.[10]

The Rules Committee replied that it could hardly be responsible for the emasculation of the appropriations bill if it contained non-privileged provisions. Chairman Smith addressed the House:

> Since I have been chairman of the Rules Committee there has been much complaint from legislative committees that the Appropriations Committee invades their field and then goes to the Rules Committee and gets a rule waiving points of order. So I made the rule that when that occurred in an appropriation bill we would do the chairman of the legislative committee the courtesy of letting him know and giving him an opportunity to be heard.[11]

In summary, three points may be made about these waivers. First, it is the Appropriations Committee that most frequently seeks such rules. Second, the number of objectionable, i.e., nonprivileged, pro-

---

[10] *Ibid.,* p. 11059. In recent years Mr. Cannon and Mr. Smith have seemed to work together more harmoniously, especially in their effort to reduce "back-door financing" by which government finances programs through Treasury borrowings rather than by congressional appropriations. However, in 1961 Cannon voted to enlarge the Committee from twelve to fifteen to give Speaker Rayburn more indirect participation in the Committee's decisions and at Judge Smith's expense, but in 1963 he voted to restore the smaller size.

[11] *Ibid.,* p. 10944.

visions within a single bill is usually small. Third, the privileged committee or the Rules Committee obtains approval from the other legislative committees whose jurisdictions may extend to the non-privileged matter.

Waivers of points of order resemble closed rules in that they give preference to the legislative committee version of a bill. Those who favor that version are pleased by the waiver; those who oppose the committee bill are likely to protest the rule. It has already been noted that the House is willing to deny itself the opportunity to amend a rather clearly prescribed class of legislation. As long as the leadership uses the closed rule within those limits, the House will follow its lead. Likewise, in certain rather well-defined cases, the House appears to understand and to consent to waiving its rights under the *Rules* to object to the presence of objectionable provisions in otherwise privileged reports.

RULES TO DISPOSE OF HOUSE-SENATE DIFFERENCES

The Committee occasionally reports rules providing for the disposition of acts that the House and Senate have passed in different versions. The House, by unanimous consent or by a special rule, either agrees to the Senate version or insists on its own form and requests a conference between representatives of both houses to resolve the outstanding differences. From the 76th to the 86th Congress (1939 to 1960) the Rules Committee reported twenty-three rules for the purpose of handling differences between the House and the Senate. One of these, a rule on a 1950 tax bill, was an issue of some controversy and was defeated on the House floor, the only such rule defeated in several decades.

This type of rule is worked out in close consultation with the party leaders. One of the most notable rules for disposing of differences between the two Houses was passed in the first session of the 85th Congress (1957), and this case illustrates several points about relations between the Rules Committee and the party leadership. In

1957 the Senate revised an omnibus civil rights act and made it largely a voting rights law. Initially, Democratic and Republican leaders in the House took quite opposite stands on how the House should dispose of the revised act. Republican strategists wanted to alter the Senate version materially, and their best chance appeared to rest with a conference committee. Democratic leaders, on the other hand, preferred to accept the Senate draft with one amendment, and they hoped the Rules Committee would report a rule to that effect.

However, for several days the Committee took no action in either direction. Chairman Smith, who was opposed to a voting rights bill in any form, would not summon a meeting. When Democratic leaders searched for Mr. Smith to request him to call his Committee together, he was reported to have rushed to his nearby dairy farm where a barn was on fire. This reputedly led Speaker Rayburn to remark, "I knew Howard Smith would do most anything to block a civil rights bill. But I never suspected he would resort to arson."[12]

Six Democrats, including two Southerners, were ready to grant the rule requested by their party's leadership, but seven votes are required to call a special meeting; and the seventh Democrat, William Colmer of Mississippi, was as opposed to the action as Chairman Smith. None of the four Republicans would provide the seventh vote for a special meeting until the Democratic leadership and its Republican counterpart agreed on a compromise. Once Speaker Rayburn and Minority Leader Martin and their fellow party leaders reached an agreement, Republican Hugh Scott (Pennsylvania) added his signature to the motion by the six Democrats for a special meeting. This was filed with the Committee Clerk at 9:30 A.M., and at 11 o'clock the same morning the Committee convened and drafted a rule. The Chairman agreed to appoint an advocate of the rule, Ray Madden (Democrat, Indiana), as floor manager, and the rule was immediately reported to the House by Mr. Madden.[13]

[12] *The New York Times,* August 21, 1957, p. 16, col. 2.

[13] See the informative dispatches of William S. White, *ibid.,* August 20 through August 27, 1957.

This case illustrates how the Committee can act as an instrument of the party leaderships when the leaders feel strongly about an issue. The compromise was not worked out in the Committee. It was agreed upon elsewhere, drafted by the Parliamentarian of the House at the behest of the leadership, and implemented by the Committee acting as agent for the leadership. Perhaps, had the Democrats not been split, they could have reported a rule of their own making and ignored Republican protests. But whether such a severe rule would have passed the House is doubtful. Had the Republican leaders firmly opposed the rule on the floor, it might well have been defeated, because the southern Democrats, who opposed any bill, would have joined the Republicans, who preferred a bill in another form.

LENGTH OF TIME FOR DEBATE

In addition to prescribing the conditions under which legislation will be considered, a rule also stipulates the length of debate. Usually the time is stated in hours, although occasionally in days. The essential difference between hours-of-debate and days-of-debate is that the former is more exact and more certain of being observed in fact as well as in spirit. An hour's debate is counted strictly as sixty minutes, where as the length of a day's debate depends on how late the House sits. Rather than accept a rule providing for a considerable number of hours of debate, those who see an advantage in a sharper restriction may prefer a limitation in terms of days, for by early adjournments they may then succeed in confining debate to a very few hours or even minutes.

As Table 6 shows, the vast majority of open rules provides for one or two hours of debate, after which the bills are read for amendment under the five-minute rule. A total of 1,128 bills was brought in under open rules during the 76th through the 86th Congresses. Of these only 132 were debated four hours or longer, and only seventy-eight provided for five hours or more of debate. About one-half the closed rules are debated for only one or two hours, whereas the other half are argued at greater length. One would expect bills under closed rules to require more debate, because a larger percentage of such measures is likely to be more controversial than those handled under open rules. Furthermore, the waiving of amendments under the five-minute rule eliminates an extra opportunity for debate.

Table 6

LENGTH OF TIME FOR DEBATE UNDER OPEN AND CLOSED RULES

(76th-86th Congresses)

LENGTH	OPEN	*Per-centage*	CLOSED	*Per-centage*
1 hour	578	*47.6*	17	*1.4*
2 hours	339	*27.9*	27	*2.2*
3 hours	79	*6.5*	11	*.9*
4 hours	54	*4.4*	9	*.7*
over 4 hours	78	*6.4*	23	*1.9*
TOTAL	1,128	*92.8*	87	*7.2*

The amount of time allotted for debate more or less varies with the controversial character of the issue and also depends on how new or routine the issue is. When an established policy is merely being reaffirmed or extended or a relatively minor issue is being resolved, the rule usually provides for only one or two hours of debate. When a new policy is at stake, however, and when the Rules Committee senses considerable division among the members, the rule is likely to allow four hours or more for debate. For example, foreign economic and military assistance, begun in the 80th Congress, was debated for twelve to fifteen hours the first two years. The length of debate declined as the program became more routine, but, owing to its controversial character, it has never been considered for less than four hours.

The House invariably accepts the Committee's recommendations for the allocation of time for debate. The Committee usually has inquired of members of both parties to determine how long they need to debate the bill, and it then provides sufficient time. If the rule is controversial, it is not because of the length of debate that is proposed.

Summary

This chapter has reviewed the use of the four kinds of rules that the Rules Committee proposes for regulating House debate and the length of time usually given for considering bills and resolutions. Closed rules, which prohibit amendments or stipulate what particular amendments may be in order, are used sparingly and mostly for considering fiscal questions. Only one closed rule has been defeated in twenty-five years. Open rules, which allow for amendment under the five-minute rule, are most frequently proposed and apply to both controversial and noncontroversial legislation. Rules waiving points of order against the inclusion of objectionable matter in otherwise privileged bills are occasionally proposed, usually at the request of the Appropriations Committee and with the concurrence of the legislative committee concerned. There are also rules for reconciling conflict between the House and Senate over the language of the same act. The length of time for debate varies with the controversy and novelty of the issue, but most debates are limited to two hours or less. Committee decisions about the allocation of time are hardly ever reviewed.

4

Committee Organization
and
Committee Decisions

the occasions for decision and the kinds of decisions that confront
the Committee. Next we turn to the organization of the Committee—
its evolution, authority, size, and relation to other institutions within
the House. The principal organizational issue involving the Committee has been whether it should function as an instrument of the
majority of the House or of the majority party and its leadership.
This issue has been at the center of three changes in the Committee's
organization and powers in the twentieth century. First, we will
briefly review the emergence of the Committee at the end of the
nineteenth century and also summarize the controversies of 1909-10,
1949-51, and 1961-63. These latter events reveal the House's expectations about the Committee's role and influence. In each case
we shall address the question, "what difference, if any, did the change
in the Committee's organization make so far as its decisions are concerned?" Then we will examine the base and means of the chairman's
power, for his is an important role in House and Committee decisions.

ORIGINS AND GROWTH

A Committee on Rules was appointed when the First Congress met in New York in April, 1789, but it was not made a standing committee until 1880[1] when the House *Rules* underwent a general revision comparable in scope to the Legislative Reorganization Act of 1946. The membership numbered five until the overthrow of Speaker Joseph G. Cannon (Republican, Illinois) in 1910, when the proposal of George Norris (Republican, Nebraska) to enlarge the Committee to ten members was adopted.[2] In 1911 an eleventh member was added;[3] a twelfth was appointed in 1917;[4] and with the exception of a brief period in the 1930's when there were fourteen,[5] the size of the Committee remained at twelve until its increase to fifteen in 1961.

The Speaker was appointed a member in 1958, when the Committee was directed to prepare a revision of the *Rules*,[6] but he was prohibited from serving by the "revolution" of 1910.[7] The Reorganization Act of 1946 removed the prohibition, but neither Joseph W. Martin, Sam Rayburn, nor John McCormack sought to take advantage of the opportunity.

[1] Asher Hinds and Clarence Cannon, *Precedents of the House of Representatives,* 11 volumes (Washington: Government Printing Office, 1907-41); Hinds, *Precedents* IV, sec. 4320; *Congressional Record,* 44th Cong., 2nd Sess., p. 205.

[2] *Congressional Record,* 61st Cong., 2nd Sess., p. 3429.

[3] *Congressional Record,* 62nd Cong., 1st Sess., p. 12 (the proposal) and p. 80 (the passage). Cannon, *Precedents* VII, sec. 2047, is in error in reporting that the Norris resolution of March 19, 1910, increased the membership from five to eleven. Norris originally proposed to increase the number to fifteen, but settled for ten. At the beginning of the next Congress the proposed *Rules* provided for eleven members, and that provision was adopted.

[4] Cannon, *Precedents* VII, sec. 2047; *Congressional Record,* 65th Cong., 1st Sess., p. 111.

[5] See annual *Congressional Directory* (Washington: Government Printing Office).

[6] Hinds, *Precedents* IV, sec. 4321.

[7] Cannon, *Precedents* VII, sec. 2047; *Congressional Record,* 61st Cong., 2nd Sess., p. 3429.

From 1789 to 1841 the Committee was authorized to report at the beginning of each Congress. Because the first *Rules,* which were drawn by an illustrious committee including Elias Boudinot (New Jersey) as Chairman, James Madison (Virginia), Roger Sherman (Connecticut), and Elbridge Gerry (Massachusetts), were customarily readopted by each Congress, the Rules Committee had virtually nothing to do. "For many years it never made a report. Indeed, so slightingly was it regarded that Speakers, during five Congresses [15th to 20th, 1817-28] neglected to appoint such a committee."[8] In 1841 the Committee was granted the right to report from time to time[9] and in 1890 to report at any time,[10] although it actually had been exercising authority of reporting at any time for several years before it was formally given that right by the House *Rules.*[11] In 1892 Rules Committee reports were designated matters of "special and high privilege" with only one motion to adjourn and no other dilatory motions in order during their considerations.[12] A year later this Committee, alone among all committees, was allowed to meet without special leave during a sitting of the House.[13]

In 1883 the House began the practice of making a special order by majority vote on a report from the Rules Committee.[14] For several years such special orders were regarded as of doubtful validity.[15] In 1887 Speaker John G. Carlisle ruled that all special orders must be referred to the Rules Committee,[16] and the House *Rules* of 1890 were made to read, "all proposed action touching the rules, joint rules, and order of business shall be referred to the Committee on Rules."[17]

[8] DeAlva Stanwood Alexander, *History and Procedure of the House of Representatives* (Boston: Houghton Mifflin Co., 1916), p. 182.

[9] Hinds, *Precedents* IV, sec. 4321.

[10] *Ibid.,* sec. 4621.

[11] *Ibid.,* p. 952, footnote 5.

[12] *Ibid.,* sec. 4621.

[13] *Ibid.,* sec. 4546.

[14] *Ibid.,* sec. 3160.

[15] *Ibid.,* p. 192, footnote 4.

[16] *Congressional Record,* 49th Cong., 2nd Sess., p. 1785.

[17] Rule XI, Clause 45, *Congressional Record,* 51st Cong., 1st Sess., p. 1106 (introduced) and p. 1347 (adopted).

It is this provision that is central to the role of the Rules Committee. The bulk of the Committee's work consists of considering resolutions concerning the order of business on the House floor, the subject matter of Chapters 2 and 3. But this bare description of the job sheds little light on what business receives preference. The very brevity of the Committee's formal assignment perhaps accounts for the periodic controversies that surround the decisions and the decision processes of the Committee.

THE REVOLT AGAINST CANNON

The first effort to amend the power of the Committee occurred during the Speakership of Joe Cannon. This little legislative tyrant was probably the last of that type of Congressional leader described in Woodrow Wilson's *Congressional Government*. Cannon believed in the doctrine of responsible parties as it has rarely been practiced in Congress or elsewhere. He used the Rules Committee as his instrument for setting and dominating the agenda of the House. He recognized members whom he knew would co-operate with him, and his eye assiduously and not so subtly avoided those who opposed him. He appointed Committees and designated their chairmen according to ruthless rules of personal favors and exchanges. His czarism became an intra-party as well as an inter-party issue, and indeed, were it not for a split in Republican ranks, the overthrow of Cannon would not have been possible in 1910.

A series of bipartisan votes extending over two years (1909-10) gradually reduced the power of the Speaker. First, Democrats and Insurgent Republicans wrote into the *Rules* provisions for the Discharge Calendar, the Unanimous Consent Calendar, and Calendar Wednesday. Then, on the crucial vote to enlarge the membership of the Rules Committee and to prohibit the Speaker from being a member of it, 149 Democrats were joined by 42 Republicans, mostly Insurgents, against 156 Republicans. By removing Cannon from the Rules Committee, the House intended to make the Committee an agent of the House majority (of whatever partisan or bipartisan alignments) as well as a sometime agent of the leadership of the majority party. The circumstances surrounding the two years of Democratic and Insurgent efforts to restrict Mr. Cannon's role clearly indicate an intent to strengthen the majority of the House (whether partisan or bipartisan) at the expense of the power of the leadership of the majority party.[18]

It would, however, be a mistake to believe that the Cannon controversy was merely a dispute over principles of Congressional organization and doctrines of responsibility. Principles and doctrines did not cause the Insurgents to depart from the regular Republicans. Kenneth W. Hechler (now a Democratic Representative from West Virginia), in his authoritative political history of the Insurgency movement, writes, "It was 'Uncle Joe' Cannon's economic and social philosophy that first aroused the western Congressmen against his autocracy. The question of power in itself did not greatly excite the average Congressman; but power exercised for reactionary economic and social ends seemed downright pernicious."[19] As Victor Murdock of Kansas told Hechler thirty years later,

> There was never anything the matter with the rules themselves; it was the way in which they were administered. Put in the speakership a man with progressive principles and your difficulties would have been immediately solved.[20]

Hechler's work, based largely upon papers, letters, and interviews of participants in the 1909-10 controversy, is supported by William R.

[18] The argument and interpretation contained in this paragraph are based on two historical works: Kenneth W. Hechler, *Insurgency: Personalities and Politics of the Taft Era* (New York: Columbia University Press, 1940); William Rea Gwinn, *Uncle Joe Cannon, Archfoe of Insurgency: A History of the Rise and Fall of Cannonism* (Ph.D. dissertation, University of Notre Dame, 1953). A similar interpretation is taken by Arthur N. Holcombe, *Our More Perfect Union: From Eighteenth-Century Principles to Twentieth-Century Practice* (Cambridge: Harvard University Press, 1950), p. 174.

[19] *Insurgency,* p. 31.

[20] *Ibid.,* p. 38.

Gwinn's study of Cannon's correspondence and other relevant manuscript sources.[21] The accumulated evidence of Hechler and Gwinn
supports the view that the overthrow of Cannon was intended to ease
the way for the majority of the House to work its will in behalf of
policies not necessarily consistent with those of the leadership.

Not only was this the expectation, but the Committee's decisions
have often favored the House majority, whatever the partisan composition of that majority. Analysis of extant data on roll-call voting
within the Committee reveals that as far back as there are records
the Committee has had as many, if not more, cross-party roll-call
decisions as it has had straight party roll-call votes. Table 7 displays
these data. Records are missing for many years of the Committee's

Table 7

**FREQUENCY OF STRAIGHT- AND CROSS-PARTY
COMMITTEE ROLL CALLS**

NUMBER AND DATE OF CONGRESS	Roll-call votes	Straight-party votes	Cross-party votes
66th: 1919-1921	10	6	4
67th: 1921-1923	10	4	6
68th: 1923-1925 (1st session)	7	3	4
69th: 1925-1927	1	0	1
70th: 1928-1929	9	5	4
74th: 1935-1936	1	0	1
75th: 1937-1938	1	0	1
80th: 1948-1950 (1st session)	3	2	1
84th: 1955-1956	4	0	4
85th: 1957-1958	12	3	9
86th: 1959-1960	12	2	10
87th: 1961-1962	11	1	10
TOTAL	81	26	55

history but are available for twenty-two years covering twelve Congresses, spanning the period 1909-1962. Only eighty-one roll-call
votes have been found, indicating that most of the Committee's decisions are taken informally and without recording individual prefer-

[21] *Uncle Joe Cannon.*

ences. But of these, more than two-thirds have involved at least one member's voting with the opposition. Such behavior is not expected from men whose vote is to serve only the majority party and its leadership; it is behavior that comports with the expectation that the Committee should also serve the majority of the House.

THE 21-DAY RULE

A major debate involving the Committee occurred after the presidential election of 1948. Harry Truman's surprise victory was accompanied by an increase in "liberal" Democratic membership in the House. Administration supporters proposed to strengthen their Congressional position by curtailing some of the authority of the Rules Committee, which the liberals looked upon as consisting of a bipartisan conservative coalition. Administration Democrats proposed the "21-Day-Rule," which provided that:

> If the Committee on Rules shall adversely report, or fail to report within 21 calendar days after reference, any resolution pending before the committee providing an order of business for the consideration by the House of any public bill or joint resolution favorably reported by a committee of the House, on days when it shall be in order to call up motions to discharge committees it shall be in order for the chairman of the committee which reported such bill or joint resolution to call up for consideration by the House the joint resolution which the Committee on Rules has so adversely reported or failed to report, and it shall be in order to move the adoption by the House of said resolution adversely reported or not reported, notwithstanding the adverse report, or the failure to report, of the Committee on Rules, and the Speaker shall recognize the members seeking recognition for that purpose as a question of the highest privilege. . . .[22]

Discharge days in the House are the second and fourth Mondays of each month. The 21-Day Rule thus gave the chairmen of legislative committees two days monthly to call up measures pigeonholed by the Rules Committee, providing the chairmen could secure recognition from the Speaker.

[22] *Congressional Record,* 81st Cong., 1st Sess., pp. 10-11.

On the opening day of the 81st Congress, Representative Sabath, adhering to the custom that the Chairman of the Rules Committee shall offer the first motion with respect to the House *Rules,* moved that the *Rules* of the 80th Congress, with the addition of the 21-Day Rule, be adopted as the *Rules* of the 81st Congress. He immediately called for the previous question, which, when approved by a voice vote, foreclosed all debate. The Democratic Party caucus had voted 176 to 48[23] to bind its membership (a two-thirds vote is necessary to bind, with the understanding that members who have made campaign commitments contrary to the caucus decision are released from the caucus bind). The Republican leadership declared against this change in the *Rules,* but both parties suffered defections. The total vote of 245 to 142 consisted of 225 Democrats, 49 Republicans, and one American Labor Party member (Vito Marcantonio, New York) in favor of the motion and 31 Democrats and 111 Republicans against.

When the second session of the 81st Congress convened in January, 1950, Representative Eugene Cox (Georgia), usually regarded as an anti-administration Democrat, proposed to repeal the 21-Day Rule. The Rules Committee, by a 9 to 2 vote (Sabath and Ray Madden, Indiana Democrat, were the minority), favorably reported the Cox amendment to the House *Rules.* After an hour's debate, the majority of Democrats, with the assistance of 64 northern Republicans, triumphed 236 to 183, but the victory was noticeably smaller than when the rule was first adopted.

This vote probably did not reflect a clear division of the House on the issue of Rules Committee power. The vote was taken on the Friday before the first Monday, when chairmen could call up bills that the Rules Committee had sidetracked. Because the Chairman of the Committee on Education and Labor was expected to attempt to call up a Fair Employment Practice measure at the earliest opportunity, southern Democrats were anxious to vote on Friday, hoping to repeal the 21-Day Rule and thus forestall possible consideration

[23] *New York Times,* January 2, 1949, p. 1, col. 1.

of FEPC on Monday. However, some Republicans who were opposed to the 21-Day Rule hesitated to put themselves in the position of appearing to oppose civil rights legislation. Therefore, it is likely that the 64 Republicans who defected from their leadership to vote to retain the 21-Day Rule included several whose votes reflected motives other than satisfaction with the rule.[24] Eighty-five Democrats broke with their party's majority and voted for repeal.

A year later, at the opening of the 82nd Congress, Sabath moved that the *Rules* of the 81st Congress be adopted for the 82nd. This motion was voted down, whereupon Cox offered a resolution that the *Rules* of the 81st Congress, minus the 21-Day Rule, be adopted. One hundred fifty-two Republicans and 92 Democrats combined to restore to the Rules Committee the authority it lost in 1949. Forty-two Republicans, 136 Democrats, and one Independent (Frazier Reams, Ohio), were in the minority. Thus, the 21-Day Rule lasted for only one term, but the controversy over its short life called forth considerable discussion about what the House expects of the Rules Committee.

An hour's debate preceded two of the three votes. The issue was phrased in several ways.[25] Those who favored a means of circumventing the Rules Committee usually took one of two tacks: either they emphasized the particular legislation the Committee seemed unwilling or unlikely to report or they took a more philosophic position that the "will of a House majority" should not be frustrated by six or seven members of a single committee, especially a committee that is not ordinarily regarded as a substantive committee. Opposition debaters rested their case on one of three major contentions. Some frankly acknowledged that they disapproved the legislation the Rules Committee was likely to defeat, and, therefore, they endorsed its authority. Others emphasized the tendency of committees to report bills they knew the House would not pass, and somebody, it was said,

[24] *New York Times,* January 21, 1950, p. 1, col. 5.

[25] The debates appear in the *Congressional Record,* 81st Cong., 2nd Sess., pp. 706-19 and 82nd Cong., 1st Sess., pp. 9-18.

must separate important from trivial matters. Still others thought a coordinating committee was necessary to prevent the House from voting billions of dollars the country could not afford. (In a year in which the total federal budget was about $40 billion, House committees were said to have approved bills, which, if all had been enacted, would have cost $67 billion.) Some members appeared to believe that a Rules Committee composed of members from safe constituencies could more conveniently resist strong, well-organized interest groups than could legislative committees or the whole House. The *New York Times* quoted an unnamed member of the Rules Committee as saying, "The Rules Committee has been 'taking the rap' in an effort to express the will of the House majority."[26]

Debaters on both sides claimed to speak on behalf of "responsible government," but their conceptions of this varied. Advocates of the 21-Day Rule thought government should be responsible to the majority sentiments of the country as reflected in a majority of the House or the majority leadership (which majority the advocates of the 21-Day Rule represented was not always clear). Opponents of the rule who talked about responsible government appeared to mean a government that abides by precepts of economy and resistance to pressure groups. But the debate exhibited virtually no consideration of how the House might need a committee to serve as a "clearing house" or "traffic light," without exercising broad discretionary authority over the content of legislation. No one came to grips with the issue: Can policy be separated from procedure? Members were more inclined to debate the issue in terms of "majority rule" (with confusion about which majority should rule) versus "socialism" (and, it might be added, with some confusion about the meaning of socialism too).

Representative Sabath, an administration supporter, Chairman of the Rules Committee, and Dean of the House, likened the fight over the 21-Day Rule to the overthrow of Speaker Cannon in 1910. Sabath had been a fledgling member of Congress when Cannon was relieved of some of his powers and expelled from the Rules Committee.

[26] December 29, 1948, p. 14, col. 7.

Sabath, who had often been unable to control his committee, insisted that the Rules Committee should be an instrument of the majority party. He interpreted the unique 8 to 4 party division of membership as a clear indication that the majority party should have an unobstructed hand at organizing the business of the House and enacting its legislative program. But because three of the eight Democrats (most frequently Eugene Cox, Howard Smith, and William Colmer) were inclined to agree with the four Republicans, "The majority has been unable to work its will." Furthermore, Sabath contended "that the membership should not be deprived of voting on any and all legislation approved and reported by committees after full and complete hearings and consideration."[27]

During the first debate Speaker Rayburn took the floor in an effort to separate the *Rules* of the House from any particular issue of policy. His remarks were especially directed toward his southern colleagues, many of whom were voting against the 21-Day Rule because they feared it would increase the chances for the passage of civil rights legislation, which they opposed. Rayburn contended that civil rights legislation was not the issue. "The rules," he said, "of a legislative body should be such at all times as to allow the majority of a legislative body to work its will."[28]

Representative Mike Monroney (Democrat, Oklahoma) answered the charge that the Rules Committee performs the necessary func-

---

[27] *Congressional Record,* 81st Cong., 2nd Sess., p. 706.

[28] *Congressional Record,* 81st Cong., 2nd Sess., p. 708. Rayburn did not speak during the second debate; the Texas member of the Rules Committee, John Lyle of Corpus Christi, supported Cox's resolution to repeal the 21-Day provision. These two facts have encouraged the inference that Rayburn was not disappointed by repeal. The inference is weak, however, because Lyle supported Cox in 1950 when the Rules Committee voted 9 to 2 to report a resolution eliminating the 21-Day Rule; only a few days later Rayburn spoke on the floor in behalf of the rule. Lewis Lapham suggests that Rayburn preferred not to possess the explicit authority that forced him to decide whether to recognize a committee chairman who wanted to by-pass the Rules Committee. Lapham also suggests that Rayburn's silence may have stemmed from his recognition that the rule would be repealed regardless of what he said. *Party Leadership and the House Committee on Rules* (Ph.D. dissertation, Harvard University, 1953).

tion of rechecking the work of the legislative committees. "Do we not trust ourselves?" he asked. "Must we have a group of twelve men on the Rules Committee to protect myself against myself, or you from yourself?" Monroney reminded the House that legislative committee chairmen going before the Rules Committee begging for a special order for the consideration of legislation their committees had previously approved have been "treated far worse than any lobbyist would be treated in the standing committees."[29]

Louis Heller (Democrat, New York) added that the Rules Committee was not intended to be the watchdog of the Treasury nor the coordinator of appropriation bills. That function, he insisted, belonged solely to the Committee on Appropriations.[30]

Representative Eberharter, the prime mover of the 21-Day Rule, asserted that the Rules Committee had been established "only for the purpose of regulating the traffic and the business of the House so we could have orderly and regular procedure."[31] "There is nothing in the rules of this House which authorizes this committee, in considering the order of business, to review or pass judgment upon the content of bills coming from the legislative committees of the House."[32]

Those who opposed the 21-Day Rule included Leo Allen (Illinois), the ranking Republican member on the Rules Committee. "The issue," declared Allen, "is whether or not the entire Truman socialistic program will succeed or be defeated. I refer especially to the socialization of medicine and the socialistic Brannan farm plan. Of course, there are about ten others."[33]

Allen frankly relied on the Rules Committee to withhold legislation that he and his colleagues opposed. But he also emphasized that means are available by which "the majority of the membership can bring any bill on the floor of the House for action."[34] Representative

---

[29] *Congressional Record*, 81st Cong., 2nd Sess., p. 710.

[30] *Ibid.*, 81st Cong., 2nd Sess., p. 712.

[31] *Ibid.*, 82nd Cong., 1st Sess., p. 12.

[32] *Ibid.*, 81st Cong., 2nd Sess., p. 711.

[33] *Ibid.*, p. 707.

[34] *Ibid.*, 82nd Cong., 1st Sess., p. 11.

Clarence Brown, prominent Ohio Republican and veteran of several terms on the Committee, assured the House that during his tenure "there has never been a single time when the Speaker of the House, whether he be a Democrat or Republican, has requested the Rules Committee to grant a rule on any legislation that such rule was not granted."[35] Representatives Cox and Charles Halleck (Republican, Indiana) agreed with Brown.[36]

Several speakers took pains to point out that the majority is in fact not powerless to act, even when confronted by a hostile Rules Committee. There exists the Discharge Petition, a procedure by which any committee may be relieved of a bill or resolution when a majority of the membership signs a notice to that effect. To sign a petition may be awkward, and members may be reluctant to sign, it was admitted, but Representative Cox chided his fellow Democrats that *they* had raised the discharge requirements from 145 members to a majority in 1935. Republican Representatives James Wadsworth (New York) and Christian Herter (Massachusetts) urged the House to use the facilities provided by Calendar Wednesday as a means of expediting business unpopular with the Rules Committee. The position taken by Herter and others was that with the Discharge Petition and Calendar Wednesday the Rules Committee could not frustrate a determined and genuine majority. At the same time, the Rules Committee could fulfill its necessary role of agenda-making. "In any orderly procedure," said Herter, "you have got to have some clearing body whether you call it a policy committee or Rules Committee. . . ."[37]

The effect of the 21-Day Rule was to make circumvention of the Rules Committee easier than either Calendar Wednesday or the Discharge Petition permitted. As Chapter 1 revealed, these latter pro-

---

[35] *Ibid.*, 81st Cong., 2nd Sess., p. 708. In interviews with party leaders in 1957 and 1958, I asked whether the Speaker had ever been denied a rule which he requested. No one would say he "never" was denied such a request, but all recognized the leadership's capacity to have its way when it was willing to insist upon its demands.

[36] *Ibid.*, 81st Cong., 2nd Sess., p. 711 and 82nd Cong., 1st Sess., p. 13.

[37] *Ibid.*, 81st Cong., 2nd Sess., p. 711.

cedures have not proved useful for conducting regular business of the House. Although only eight bills passed the House under the 21-Day Rule, they were issues of great import. The essential difference between the 21-Day Rule and Calendar Wednesday and the Discharge Petition is the burden of taking the initiative. The leadership actively moves to dispense with Calendar Wednesday and members have to rebel against the leadership to restore the use of that procedure. The Discharge Petition requires the majority to take the initiative to work its will. But the 21-Day Rule allowed a committee chairman, who is part of the leadership but rather toward the periphery of it, to initiate a motion to call up his bill. The 21-Day Rule, in appearance, should have made it easier for the majority to work its will, whatever that will might be. But legislative committee chairmen still had to reckon with the Speaker, whose role allows him to yield the floor to whomever he pleases, irrespective of who rises first. As William S. White, then Congressional correspondent for the *New York Times,* wrote,

> . . . it is customary in the House for those seeking the Speaker's official ear on the floor to go to him in advance, perhaps the day before, and privately advise him as to what is afoot. Persons not taking these preliminary dispositions, which are, of course, in the nature of provisional requests, rarely get very far when the hour for recognition arrives.[38]

The Democratic leadership resisted this interpretation of the 21-Day Rule. Majority Leader McCormack took pains to say on the floor that he understood the rule to state explicitly that the Speaker "shall" recognize a committee chairman who seeks to call up a measure that the Rules Committee has ignored for twenty-one days. Under questioning McCormack held that the recognition was mandatory, even if the Speaker should oppose calling up the bill. However, the Majority Leader's reply to a colloquy of Representative Halleck seemed to cut some ground from under his own interpretation.

[38] January 9, 1949, IV, p. 5, col. 7.

Of course, as my friend knows, in practical operation the chairman of a committee would come to me as Majority Leader and ask me to program it. . . . I am sure they would come to the leadership to see about programming any proposed legislation before exercising the high privilege that is now theirs under the rules as amended.[39]

In January, 1950, on the Monday after the move to repeal the 21-Day Rule was defeated, the Committee on Education and Labor was prepared and expected to call up FEPC. However, between the Friday vote on repeal and Monday, arrangements were made with the Committee on Public Lands for its chairman to call up a resolution to admit Hawaii and Alaska to statehood. The Speaker then recognized not Chairman John Lesinski (Democrat, Michigan), of the Education and Labor Committee, but Chairman Hardin Peterson (Democrat, Florida) of the Public Lands Committee.

In summary, the debates on the 21-Day Rule, just as the controversy over Cannonism, revealed a clash over whether the Rules Committee should act as a clearing house and agenda-making group, as the agent of the leadership of the majority party, or as an agent of the Whole House that would intuitively feel the "pulse of the House" and review and edit the work of the legislative committees.

The effect of the 21-Day Rule was to increase the power of the Speaker. Forty years before, Mr. Cannon was shorn of authority and an independent Rules Committee was delegated part of the agenda-making decisions as agent of the House. In 1910 the House majority, consisting of Insurgent Republicans and Democrats, trusted a committee of ten more than a "Czar" of one. At mid-century the majority of the House (again consisting of members of both parties) temporarily preferred to balance the authority of twelve by trusting further discretion to the Speaker.

"PACKING" THE COMMITTEE

The third major controversy involving the Committee occurred in 1961 when the House, by a five-vote margin, enlarged ("packed," said the opposition) the membership from twelve to fifteen for the

[39] *Congressional Record,* 81st Cong., 2nd Sess., p. 103.

duration of the 87th Congress. By this action, the Democratic leadership appointed two new members on whom it could depend to offset Judge Smith and Mr. Colmer, who frequently voted with the Republicans against Democratic-sponsored bills. The party ratio then became ten from the majority and five from the minority.

This fight began brewing as early as 1958. A small but vocal group of Democrats who constituted the Democratic Study Group complained to Speaker Rayburn about the Rules Committee alliance, which frustrated housing, civil rights, labor, and similar social welfare legislation. At the beginning of the 86th Congress in January, 1959, Mr. Rayburn offered his personal assurance that such measures would not be bottled up in the Committee and, in exchange for this promise, the liberal Democrats withdrew any move to reform the Committee.[40] Their efforts could not have succeeded without the Speaker's support, and Rayburn's word meant more to most Congressmen than any rulebook language. But no sooner did Rayburn give his promise than he lost the one ally who could have helped him make good his assurance. Joe Martin, long the House Republican leader, was upset by Charles Halleck in a surprise vote, 74 to 70. Martin and Rayburn had served together for decades and had alternated the Speakership through the forties and fifties, and their personal friendship surpassed any partisan differences. Rayburn could always count on Martin to secure whatever number of Republican votes was needed to override Smith and Colmer and get a bill to the House floor.

When Halleck replaced Martin, Rayburn lost his trump card. The Speaker's relations with the new Republican leader were cordial but less personal and more partisan than they had been with Martin. Halleck's partisan belligerence and his unconcealed cultivation of the alliance with Howard Smith made him a different kind of antagonist.

As a result, Democratic liberals and the leadership once more were pained to see the Rules Committee interfere with what they

[40] *Chicago Sun-Times,* January 4, 1959, p. 20, col. 1.

"I Said I Had Him Trained—Notice How He Sits Up?"
—*Herblock in The Washington Post.*

73

regarded as the majority will of the House. During the 1960 presidential campaign, three cases illustrated the conflict between the Committee and its critics:

A bill to raise the minimum wage did not pass Congress because House and Senate conferees could not agree on a compromise; the discretion of the House members of the conference committee was limited because they were not appointed until the Rules Committee exacted a promise that they would not agree to more than $1.15 an hour—rather than the $1.25 demanded by sponsors of the legislation.[41]

An aid-to-education bill that had passed the House and Senate in different forms did not become law because the Rules Committee refused to grant a rule that would send the bill to a conference committee.[42]

An omnibus housing bill was passed by the Senate and favorably reported by the House Committee on Banking and Currency, but the House could not consider it because the Rules Committee would not grant it a rule.[43]

Although the responsibility for the defeat of these three bills rested with no single person or committee, the Rules Committee was heavily involved in each instance. If the Rules Committee had imposed no unusual limits on the discretion of the House conferees, the probability of enacting the minimum wage bill would have increased. If the Rules Committee had approved, an aid-to-education bill might have passed, although the President might have vetoed it. If the Rules Committee had approved, the House most probably would have passed the omnibus housing bill.

Such decisions infuriated House liberals. When one of them, a first-term Representative from Wisconsin, criticized Judge Smith on

[41] H.R. 12677.
[42] H.R. 10128.
[43] H.R. 12603.

a Washington radio program, the Judge was provoked to scold him from the floor of the House. And when a pet bill of Smith's came up for a vote, a bill that would reimburse many of his constituents for having to move to make way for the new Dulles Airport near Washington, it nearly failed of passage. Such matters are almost invariably passed by the House with little or no controversy. The closeness of the vote was attributed to many members' dissatisfaction with the Judge's behavior.[44]

Meanwhile, the Democratic Convention platform included a passage committing the party to do something about the Rules Committee. Although Senator Kennedy refrained from taking a position on altering the Committee's role, he blamed several legislative defeats on the Committee coalition. Vice-President Nixon gave a campaign promise that he would not favor changing the composition or powers of the Committee.[45]

As soon as the election was over, the Democratic Study Group and other complainants opened fire on the Committee. Documents were circulated among Democratic House members identifying the scope and extent of the Committee's power and discussing alternative modes of reform.[46] Speaker Rayburn kept his own counsel, told the President-elect this was a matter for the House, and at times appeared indecisive. There was, however, no doubt in the Speaker's mind that he would do something to curb Judge Smith and his coalition. The doubt was about *how* to do it.

Two kinds of proposals were broached between election day and the convening of the 87th Congress. One kind could be effected among the Democrats themselves; the other would require changes in the rules of the House. Those proposals, which were largely within the discretion of the Democratic caucus, included the election of

[44] Tom Wicker, "Again That Roadblock in Congress," *New York Times Magazine,* August 7, 1960, p. 68.

[45] *New York Times,* September 21, 1960, p. 22, col. 4.

[46] Democratic Study Group, "Analysis of Proposals to Overcome Legislative Obstruction by the Rules Committee," October 26, 1960; "Opposition in the House of Representatives to a Change in the Rules," October 20, 1960; "Memorandum on Sending House Bills to Conference," September 30, 1960 (all mimeographed).

**"Let 'Em Vote for Congressmen—Long as We Can
Keep the Congressmen From Voting for Them"**
—*Herblock in The Washington Post.*

members of the Rules Committee rather than their appointment by strict adherence to seniority. A less drastic version of this extraordinary alternative was to replace Colmer but leave Smith as Chairman. Such a departure from the seniority principle was too radical for many members. Although the seniority system is widely criticized outside Congress, it is generally favored within. Moreover, dumping Colmer because he had campaigned against the Kennedy-Johnson ticket would have been embarrassing; in 1956 Adam Clayton Powell (Democrat, New York) had defected to support Eisenhower-Nixon against Stevenson-Kefauver, and without any loss of seniority or committee position in the House. Citing this precedent, Colmer's supporters asked whether there was one rule for a Negro and another for whites?

Another intra-party tactic, for which there was precedent, was to give the Democrats nine members and limit the Republicans to three seats. The eight-to-four division had been worked out in a gentleman's agreement between Rayburn and Martin many years before, when Martin was the Republican leader. Martin's defeat by Halleck had released the Speaker from his part of the bargain, but the Democrats lost more than twenty seats, and it would have been difficult to justify changing the ratio under such circumstances.

Among the changes that would have required action by the whole House, the first to be mentioned was always a return to the 21-Day Rule. But it was also the first rejected, both among the Democratic liberals, the leadership, and throughout the House.

Some attention was given to changing the procedures for handling Congressional differences on the same bill. That is, the Rules Committee might be denied its participation in decisions to send bills to conference committees. Indeed, at one point, Smith seemed willing to compromise by yielding this authority in exchange for maintaining the size and composition of the Committee; but Rayburn refused to compromise.

In the end, however, the alternatives boiled down to purging Colmer or enlarging the Committee. After first deciding to remove the Mississippi defector, Rayburn shifted his strategy, and the Democratic caucus ordered the Rules Committee to report a resolution increasing its membership from twelve to fifteen. This resolution was scheduled for a vote on January 27; but the Democratic leadership feared defeat, and the vote was postponed until January 31. Meanwhile, White House aides of the President, the President's brother from the Justice Department, the Vice-President, numerous Senators, and many pressure group representatives became involved. The Speaker made the contest a matter of personal privilege and called on the enormous reservoir of affection and respect he had earned throughout a half-century in the House. At noon on the day of the vote, as he approached the rostrum in the House chamber, colleagues from both sides of the aisle stood, and the packed galleries gave him a round of admiring applause. At the end of the tense roll call, the House had voted to enlarge the Rules Committee "during the 87th Congress."[47]

What was the effect of this decision on the House's intentions for the Committee's role? By this vote, the House resolved that the Rules Committee should give priority to the preferences of the leadership of the majority party. Its status independent of the leadership was repudiated. In the continuing conflict between the roles of representing the majority party or the majority of the House, the former had won. Through its leadership the Committee was to be an arm of the majority party.

Like the 21-Day Rule, the enlargement decision strengthened the Speaker and the central forces of the majority party. Once again the House pendulum swung back toward a strong role for the leadership. Cannonism would never return in the person of Sam Rayburn,

[47] For accounts of the enlargement, see *Congressional Record,* 87th Cong., 1st Sess., January 31, 1961, daily edition, pp. 1502-19; Milton C. Cummings, Jr., and Robert L. Peabody, "The Decision to Enlarge the House Committee on Rules: An Analysis of the Vote," July, 1961, and September, 1962 (both mimeographed); C. Dwight Dorough, *Mr. Sam* (New York: Random House, 1962), Chap. 1; and especially Neil MacNeil, *Forge of Democracy: The House of Representatives* (New York: David McKay Co., 1963), Chap. 15.

but the Committee on Rules was on notice not to obstruct the Speaker in the guise of representing the will of the House.

If such was the *intention* of the House, how did the enlargement actually work? Did it serve the functions prescribed to it? First, consider the number of hearings requested but not granted in the 86th and 87th Congresses. In 1959-60 the Rules Committee refused thirty-one requests for hearings, and in 1960-61 it refused twenty-one. Second, compare the number of rules denied after hearings and the record is the same both before and after the reform, eleven. Third, the Committee continued to use its power to bargain with legislative committees about the form of the bill in exchange for a rule. This was done on an education bill, which could not go to conference without a rule; but before the Rules Committee would grant a rule it exacted of Adam Clayton Powell (Democrat, New York) and Edith Green (Democrat, Oregon) promises that they would not assent to certain portions of the Senate bill. In these respects the reform seemed to have little effect.

Fourth, the Committee increased the use of the closed rule, reporting as many in the 87th Congress (twenty-two) as it had in the 85th and 86th combined. This may reflect the new integration with the leadership, but it could also be explained by the greater volume of House business and by the scope of issues—several tax bills—considered.

Fifth, the House reversed the Committee only once, but then in a dramatic and unusual way. For the first time in twenty-five years the House defeated a closed rule. A bill to increase postal rates was brought in with the recommendation that no amendments be in order, but the House refused this by a vote of 222 to 142. Actually the Rules Committee originally voted an open rule, but one member misunderstood his signals from the leadership and voted "wrong" in committee. Later in the day he requested a reconsideration of the rule before it was filed, and Judge Smith consented. The closed rule was then reported.

As the date approached for convening the 88th Congress in January, 1963, the issue of committee size was reopened. The resolution increasing membership from twelve to fifteen had applied only to the 87th Congress, and unless further action was taken membership of the committee would revert to twelve members. However, the 1963 controversy was quickly and decisively resolved by vote of 235 to 196 in favor of making the enlargement "permanent"; i.e., the size would remain at fifteen until some contrary action was taken by a House majority.

The clear-cut victory by those who favored a fifteen-man committee closely affiliated with the leadership seemed a product of at least three principal factors. First, the balance of partisan forces in the House was not much changed by the election of 1962. For whatever reasons may have been, the Democratic majority did not suffer the diminution usual at mid-term Congressional elections. Second, as already noted, the larger-sized committee had not made much "objective" difference in the conduct of House business. The fears of 1961 had not been realized, so that those who argued for fifteen members could assert that they were seeking to maintain the status quo. Third, the three new members (Democrats Elliott of Alabama, Sisk of California, and Avery of Kansas) were well-liked and had surrendered especially good committee positions to take the thankless jobs on the Rules Committee. If dropped from Rules, they would have to begin at the bottom rung on other committees. In the absence of some overriding consideration, some members were reluctant to penalize these men who had undertaken a difficult chore. These reasons combined to maintain the Committee size at fifteen.

In respects mentioned in relation to the manner in which enlargement functioned, the weight of the Committee's power seems not to have been altered much. The scope of its rejection of hearings and rules still extends especially to education bills. Here the issues of federal intervention and Catholic-Protestant conflict combined through Democrats James Delaney (New York), James Trimble (Arkansas), and Carl Elliott (Alabama) to deny the leadership the votes it needed to report education bills. The largest number of rejections pertained to bills from the Committee on Education and Labor.

THE CHAIRMAN'S POWER

The Chairman's capacity to participate in Committee and House decisions with the probability of affecting the outcome of the decisions is a combination of his personal skills, the traditions surrounding the Chairman's role, and the extent of his general agreement with the Committee.

Since the Democrats won control of the House as a result of the election of 1930, there have been five chairmen of the Rules Committee. Edward Pou (North Carolina), whose legislative service began in 1901, presided from 1931 until his death early in 1934. He was succeeded by John J. O'Connor (New York), who was a skillful legislator, more conservative than the New Deal President of his period, an unsuccessful candidate for Majority Leader against Sam Rayburn in 1937, and the only victim of FDR's election purge-attempts of 1938. O'Connor and President Roosevelt did not see eye to eye on a number of New Deal issues, and the President countered O'Connor's intransigence by intervening in the Democratic primary and helping to deny him renomination. O'Connor subsequently ran for his seat on the Republican ticket (he had defeated Allen Dulles in the Republican primary) and barely missed winning re-election.

He was succeeded by Adolph Sabath (Illinois), who would go down the line for virtually anything the Roosevelt Administration desired. He was, however, an ineffective Chairman, unable to lead his Committee, frequently at odds with the House leadership, and inclined to write the President little letters "informing" on Speaker Bankhead and Sam Rayburn. Sabath's tenure as Chairman lasted from 1939 until his death in 1952, except for the two years of the 80th Congress (1947-48). His twelve years in the Chairmanship earned him the honor of holding that post longer than any other person in the modern history of the Committee. Otherwise he filled it without distinction. He maintained only a skeleton staff in Washington, while assigning several nominal committee employees to his

Chicago office and allowing a Washington staff member to live in the committee rooms in the Capitol Building. Records of committee decisions were kept haphazardly when at all, and many were not retained from year to year. When Committee closets were cleaned of Sabath's effects several years after his death, Committee records were found mixed among personal papers, including racing and betting information and telephone bills of calls to tracks along the East Coast.

Leo Allen (Illinois) served two terms as Chairman when Republicans organized the 80th and 83rd Congresses (1947-48, 1953-54). When he first was elected to Congress, Allen roomed with Joe Martin, was very much a regular Republican, and was closely integrated to the leadership and the Policy Committee.[48] During the Eisenhower Administration, he went to the White House for weekly meetings between the President and the legislative leaders.

When the Democrats regained control of the House in the 84th Congress (1954), Howard Worth Smith of Fauquier County, Virginia, assumed the Chairmanship. By then he had been on the Committee exactly twenty years; the years of service accumulated since that time mark him as the member with the longest tenure on the Committee since it was reconstituted in 1910. Smith was elected to the Committee in 1933 over the opposition of the newly elected Speaker, Henry Rainey (Illinois), and as something of a concession to the losing forces within the Democratic Party, a fact recalled in irony by Sam Rayburn and John McCormack in 1961 when Smith accused them of packing his Committee.

Judge Smith (he was a district judge prior to his election to Congress) fits many of the stereotypes of southern Congressmen. He still lives in the home occupied by his mother during the War Between the States when Union soldiers trooped across the family farm en route to Richmond. He was educated in a military academy and later in law at the University of Virginia. His business interests run to banking, farming, and dairying. Until World War II he wore

[48] David B. Truman, *The Congressional Party: A Case Study* (New York: John Wiley & Sons, Inc., 1959), p. 235.

wing-tip collars. He was an admirer of Roosevelt in 1932, but when F.D.R. reversed his fiscal policies, Smith, like Byrd, George, and others, parted company; in 1938 Roosevelt tried unsuccessfully to purge him. He supported O'Connor against Rayburn for the Majority Leadership in 1937. He was author of the Alien Registration Act of 1940, co-author of the Smith-Connally Labor Act, a vigilant critic of OPA, and in recent years has tried, without avail, to restrict the Supreme Court's powers to declare certain acts of state legislatures unconstitutional.

He believes the Constitution was an "inspired" document, but he doubts the validity of the Fourteenth Amendment, and at a Committee hearing he once indicated he thought the Seventeenth Amendment to elect Senators directly rather than to appoint them by the state legislatures had been a mistake. His rhetoric is that of the traditional southern Democrat:

> I will not pledge my support blindfolded to any unknown measures, to any person, or any subject, but will use my best judgment and discretion after careful study and concentration, and vote for such measures as I believe to be in the interest of the welfare of our country and in conformity with the wishes of my constituents.
>
> My views are not original with me. They are bred in the bone, nurtured through generations in you and me in this section of Virginia from whose soil came those great statesmen of the past who, with their God-given inspiration, founded and started on its historical course the greatest nation in all the history of mankind.

His district is the one which James Madison represented in the First Congress; and Madison was also a member of the first Rules Committee. It is the district that was the home of Washington, Jefferson, Marshall, Henry, Monroe, Zachary Taylor, and Robert E. Lee.

This prototype of the southern gentlemen in politics is regarded as the captain of the informal coalition of conservative Democrats from the South. His wry and earthy humor occasionally adds color to his Committee's meetings, but ordinarily he gives the disarming appearance of a sleepy, silent man, moving softly about the House floor, his mind seemingly miles away on philosophic matters.

Judge Smith is universally acknowledged as an able parliamentarian, one of two or three of the keenest in modern times. His knowledge of the *Rules* probably nearly matches that of Clarence Cannon (Democrat, Missouri), who codified them, and his experience with the Rules has likely been equaled only by the late Sam Rayburn. But his personal charm and parliamentary skills account for only part of his contemporary influence. The mere fact of being Chairman confers upon him the extraordinary opportunities for affecting legislation that only a Chairman enjoys. With his skills and long hours of work he has used these opportunities as no previous Rules Chairman has.[49]

As Chairman of the Committee, Judge Smith can usually perform a number of leadership functions without consulting his colleagues. A Committee majority could direct the Chairman to perform his role differently, but only in rare instances would it do so. Here are some of the things the Chairman can do within very broad limits, things that contribute to the policy decisions of Congress.

He calls meetings of the Committee. Although the House *Rules* stipulate that each standing committee shall have a regular meeting day,[50] the Rules Committee has never established one. This is partly because its business depends on the unpredictable order in which legislative committees seek rules for their bills. In the absence of fixed times for meeting, it is within the Chairman's discretion to determine when to call the committee together. When the Chairman opposes a particular bill, he can delay its consideration by not convening his Committee, unless his colleagues resort to a formal peti-

[49] For materials on Smith, see Raymond Moley, "Smith of Virginia," *Newsweek,* August 25, 1958, p. 80; "An Address Delivered by Hon. Harry F. Byrd . . ." *Congressional Record,* May 5, 1959, p. A3714 (daily edition); Frank Eleazer, "Vanishing Smith," *Washington Post,* August 8, 1959; "No. 2 Man in the House," *New York Times,* August 23, 1960; Audrey Graves, "Judge Smith Has a One-Sided Interest in Those Cows," *Washington Post,* September 11, 1960; "Rep. Smith Says He's Still Neutral," *Washington Post,* October 13, 1960; "The Keeper of the Rules," CBS-TV, January 19, 1961.

[50] Rule XI, clause 24.

tion and follow prescribed steps. Late in a session especially, this form of negative action can give him a veto over some controversial measures.

He decides whether to proceed without a quorum. Although Committee meetings are, according to House *Rules,* supposed to proceed only when a certain number is present, including at least one member of each party, the Chairman can conveniently suggest that business be conducted regardless of the number present. This is, of course, usually done on noncontroversial matters, and Judge Smith especially is fair to members who express an interest in a particular measure by not acting on it in their absence. While the Chairman can sometimes facilitate action by ignoring the absence of a quorum, he can also delay action by studiously observing the absence of quorum when he is opposed to a measure. Thus, on civil rights, Smith and Representative Colmer have several times played a little duet, in which Colmer notes the absence of a quorum and Smith raps his gavel to adjourn.

Likewise, in exceptional circumstances, he can physically make a quorum. For example, late one evening at the end of a long summer session of Congress, the Senate returned a foreign aid appropriation bill with amendments. It was different from the House version, so unanimous consent was required for the House to appoint conferees to adjust differences. However, an objection was heard, and the only alternative was for the Rules Committee to meet, report out a rule, and allow the House to act by majority vote. Judge Smith arose on the floor of the House, announced he was calling an executive session of the Rules Committee upstairs in its rooms, and requested that his colleagues follow him there. When they convened, Representatives Colmer and Budge protested the rule; and when they observed that their absence would leave the Committee without a quorum, they retired to a connecting room. When they refused to return, Judge Smith led his colleagues into the room where Colmer and Budge had retreated, declared a quorum present, entertained a motion to report the necessary rule, and at 11:15 P.M. returned to the House floor to call up the rule to send the bill to conference.

He sets the agenda. It falls to the Chairman to determine when and in what order bills will be heard. The typical procedure is that when legislative committees report bills, their chairmen request hearings from the Rules Committee. On highly salient issues, the House leadership may urge a hearing. But it is in the Chairman's discretion precisely when the hearing will be held. There are always enough pending requests for hearings that the Chairman can conveniently schedule bills he favors and postpone those he opposes, thus delaying consideration of some matters. Some chairmen of the Rules Committee have been known to smother the Committee's agenda with relatively minor legislation as a way of postponing items that they personally oppose. After the enlargement of the Committee in 1961, Judge Smith began sharing with the Committee more decision-making about its agenda. From time to time, he reviewed with his colleagues the pending business and asked for their views on what should be considered and in what order.

He schedules witnesses. Although the Committee ordinarily hears only members of the House, the Chairman may on occasion call special witnesses, such as Senators, officials in the executive branch, or even representatives of particular groups who are interested in legislation before the Committee. However, the Chairman's power derives not so much from his power to schedule witnesses from outside the House as it does from his opportunity to encourage other members of the House to appear before his Committee and delay Committee action on a bill he opposes. For example, in the spring of 1957, Judge Smith obviously did not discourage southern members of Congress from queuing up to testify about the civil rights bill. Even when the testimony became redundant, he could in all fairness plead that he should not cut off his distinguished colleagues who had waited so patiently and for so long to tell the Committee about the pending bill. The opposition's testimony was of much greater length than that of the proponents; indeed, the proponents of the bill deliberately stayed away from the Committee in order not to slow down Committee consideration.

Once again, it should be noted that this power of the Chairman is essentially a negative one. He can find witnesses to oppose bills, but he cannot facilitate legislation by calling favorable witnesses; on the other hand, he can facilitate action by indicating that in his view no further testimony is required.

He decides when to put an issue to a vote. Although, technically, any member of the Committee can move to report a bill, the Chairman often specifies what bills he would like to consider for possible reporting. Only then do members usually make motions on particular bills. As a result, the Chairman can further delay decision or facilitate action according to his preferences. In 1958, Chairman Smith never did put the Alaska statehood bill to a vote, and no member of the Committee ever moved that it be reported. As a result, consideration by the House was delayed until the bill was brought to the floor by a rarely used procedure under which the Committee on Interior and Insular Affairs is privileged to call up statehood bills without a special order from Rules. Professor George Peek of the University of Michigan, who has retraced the long history of Alaska's campaign for statehood, believes that a favorable decision on admission might have been obtained ten years earlier but for the Rules Committee's opposition, executed so skillfully by its Chairman.[51]

He reports the Committee's resolutions to the House and then calls them up for consideration, or assigns this function to another member of the Committee. In earlier days of the Committee's history, the Chairman might refuse to file a rule even after the Committee voted to report it. However, since 1923, when the House *Rules* were amended to require him to report the rule within a certain number of days, chairmen have not abused this privilege. Nevertheless, some power remains, for the Chairman may assign a rule to a Committee member who actually opposes the rule, in which case time on the rule can be used to criticize the bill. On the other hand, the Chairman can facilitate passage of the rule by giving it to a member who is favorably disposed toward it. Further, the Chairman may help or hinder a member's relations with his constituency by the rules he

[51] See the forthcoming monograph by George Peek to be published by the Inter-University Case Program.

gives him to call up. For example, in 1961 Judge Smith assigned the rule to enlarge the Committee to Judge Trimble, whose constituency was about to be redistricted because of Arkansas' loss of population. As Trimble noted in calling up the rule, this was not an assignment he had sought.

He serves as the center of communications to the Committee. Communications coming to and from the Committee about legislative committee requests for hearings and about the views of members of the Rules Committee center around the Chairman. As previously noted, the Chairman receives requests for rules from other committees and from the majority party leadership. No other member, not even the ranking minority member, usually keeps a file of bills on which hearings and action have been requested. In fact, until Clarence Brown (Ohio) became senior Republican on the Committee, there was no minority staff person permanently assigned to the Committee. The Chairman usually does not pass information about scheduling and requests to his colleagues or to the leadership except when it is sought. When Leo Allen was Chairman during the 83rd Congress, he periodically circulated lists of pending bills, but Judge Smith put a stop to that. This near monopoly of information reinforces the Chairman's traditional authority to set his own pace in calling meetings and taking votes. Inasmuch as it is the Chairman's office that calls all committee members before a meeting, the Chairman is much more likely than his colleagues to know whether and when it is to his advantage to vote on certain issues.

These powers of the Chairman are mostly negative. The Chairman, like the Committee, is more favorably situated to veto legislation than to promote it. To be sure, Judge Smith has, through his position, brought his H. R. 3 within one Senate vote of adoption, but only once, and he has not been able to repeat that near-success. Occasionally the Chairman, like the Committee, can give an assist to a bill, but more often his influence in the House and in national politics is to veto, amend, or legitimate rather than to initiate or originate action.

5

Organizational Experience, Constituency Backgrounds, and Committee Decisions

analyzed the kinds of decisions and occasions for decision before the Committee. Chapter 4 described the organizational context—the House's expectations—in which the Committee has operated through recent history. We now move to a third set of factors that should enhance our understanding of the Committee. This chapter reports individual data on members of the Rules Committee for the period 1937-62 and considers the relationship between certain of their individual characteristics and the decision-making process and policy outcomes in the House of Representatives.

From my observation of Congressmen—through interviews, listening to debates, attending hearings, working beside them—at least two major "motives" or personal characteristics seem to be important, one organizational and the other nonorganizational.[1] The former is

---

[1] I am, of course, aware of my loose use of the terms "motive" and "personal characteristic." In general, this usage follows that of Richard C. Snyder, H. W. Bruck, and Burton Sapin, *Foreign Policy Decision-Making* (New York: The Free Press of Glencoe, 1962), pp. 137-71. Especially see pp. 155-58, where norms and values internal to the decision unit are distinguished from those that are external to the total decision-making structure and internalized in the decision-maker.

a predisposition to be in the majority or at least with the leadership of one's party; the latter relates to the tendency to satisfy elements, especially constituents, external to the organization. These are not necessarily incompatible, because favors from the party leadership may help one's district, but there are numerous occasions when one's party and constituent interests differ.

There is a widespread awareness among politicians of an epigram attributed to the late Speaker Sam Rayburn: "To get along, go along." Many a Congressman adopts this for his philosophy, not grudgingly, but with the conviction that if he is to get things done, this is his best strategy. Even public officials with strong beliefs come to reconcile themselves with "the organization." They move to Washington ready to bend every effort to achieve the programs they espoused in their election campaigns. But soon they learn that some of the interests of their constituents are in conflict with groups represented by other members of Congress. To insist on everything for one's own group seems to net nothing. In time one learns that the effective leaders in both houses of Congress, i.e., the ones who can mobilize sufficient support to obtain some of their legislative ends, are the members who co-operate with all reasonable men, who give and take, who trade, barter, and deal, who bargain and compromise.

It is true that not all legislators follow the lead; some indeed rebel against the organization.[2] And a few, like George Norris and Robert La Follette, live to see their views belatedly accepted by Congress. Their operating theory, more recently articulated by Senator Paul Douglas (Democrat, Illinois), is that they will have influence *on* Congress but not *in* Congress. Other legislators must deviate from the organizational norm in order to meet the needs of their constituents. One of the striking things about Congress, as about other elective bodies, is that the talents for being elected may not neces-

[2] For perceptive studies of legislators who deviate from typical organizational patterns, see Ralph K. Huitt, "The Outsider in the Senate: An Alternative Role," *American Political Science Review*, 55 (1961), 566-75, and A. Robert Smith, *The Tiger in the Senate: The Biography of Wayne Morse* (Garden City, N. Y.: Doubleday and Co., Inc., 1962).

sarily be the same as the talents for being an "effective" member after election.[3]

The desire to continue to represent one's constituency is, thus, a second major motive for most public officials. Former Speaker Joseph W. Martin (Republican, Massachusetts) has said, "No one can fully understand the motives of any member of Congress without knowing something about his district."[4] Most politicians presumably like the work and hence are pleased to fulfill constituency obligations. They realize that the electorate chose them to represent their views when known. Politicians also know that he who departs too much from the known views of the people at home will not likely be given further opportunity to do so. Where the strongly-expressed expectations of the constituency conflict with the majority feeling of Congress, constituency will usually prevail. And this is sanctioned by tradition among party leaders. As one veteran House leader pointedly asserted, "It would be *morally wrong, morally wrong* to ask a man to destroy himself politically."[5]

The problem of probing the motivations of the fifty-three men who sat on the Rules Committee from 1937 through 1962 is so formidable that no reader will expect anything approaching a complete explanation, given the present state of knowledge and the obvious difficulties in learning important personal characteristics of public servants. It is, however, possible to organize some relevant data around the "organizational" motive and the "constituency" motive. We shall see what can be learned about the kind of men who are put on this Committee by looking into their previous Congressional experience; and non-organizational motivations may be enlightened by analysis of the constituency backgrounds of legislative decision-makers. The basic

[3] On the relationship between requirements for nomination and election as distinguished from requirements for office in the case of the presidency, see my "Rationality and Decision-Making: The Illinois Democratic Delegation," in Paul Tillett, ed., *Inside Politics: The National Conventions, 1960* (Dobbs Ferry, N. Y.: Oceana Publications, Inc., 1962), pp. 240-51.

[4] Joseph W. Martin, Jr., as told to Robert J. Donovan, *My First Fifty Years in Politics* (New York: McGraw-Hill, 1960), p. 53.

[5] For another leader's similar view, see *ibid.*, pp. 246-47.

assumption is an old and familiar one: "Where a man comes from" is somehow significant in determining his views and behavior. Experience, in other words, contributes to an individual's frame of reference, through which he observes, analyzes, and reacts to the world about him. Biographers and historians have long employed this form of inquiry in their studies of individual men. Political scientists, interested in the general and typical characteristics of many men rather than the unique attributes of one man, find social background analysis useful for understanding certain kinds of political behavior. After summarizing the patterns of organizational and constituent backgrounds, we shall discuss their implications for the Committee's decisions and the policies of the House.

ORGANIZATIONAL EXPERIENCE

Prior Congressional Service. As Table 8 indicates, more than half the members had not been assigned to the Rules Committee until their third or fourth terms. It is rare for a freshman Congressman to be appointed to this Committee. John O'Connor (Democrat, New York), joined the Committee in 1923, but he was the only one of the fifty-three who was assigned at the beginning of his first session. Roger Slaughter (Democrat, Missouri) was made a member midway in his first term when a senior member died. John McSweeney (Democrat, Ohio) and James J. Delaney (Democrat, New York) were favored with Committee memberships in 1949 during their first terms after interruption of previous service in Congress.

It is almost as rare to be assigned to the Committee *after* one's third or fourth term as it is *before*. Only thirteen of the fifty-three moved to Rules in their fifth terms or later. At the personal request of the Speaker, James W. Trimble (Democrat, Arkansas) gave up a high position on the Public Works Committee in his sixth term. James W. Wadsworth (Republican, New York), William J. Driver (Democrat, Arkansas), and Carl Elliott (Democrat, Alabama) were beginning their seventh terms when the leadership summoned them

Table 8

NUMBER OF THE MEMBERS' TERMS OF SERVICE IN WHICH THEY WERE ASSIGNED TO THE COMMITTEE ON RULES, 1937-62

1st	4*
2nd	7**
3rd	11
4th	18***
5th	4
6th	1
7th	3
8th	1
10th	1
11th	2
13th	1
TOTAL	53

* Two who were appointed in their first terms had been members of Congress at previous terms, but not the immediately preceding term. Nonconsecutive service does not permit accumulated seniority, except that first-termers with prior, interrupted service rank above first-termers with no prior service.
** Three who were appointed in their second terms had prior congressional experience.
*** Two who were appointed in their fourth terms had prior congressional experience.

to duty on the Rules Committee. Wadsworth made the change in 1947 when the Republicans took control of the House for the first time since 1930. Other Republican appointees in the 80th Congress had rather long service records and were well known in Republican circles—including Ross Rizley (Oklahoma) and Christian Herter (Massachusetts)—which meant that the Republican leadership had a basis for knowing whether these were members on whom it could rely for co-operation in arranging a legislative program. In 1961 the Republicans called Katherine St. George (New York) in her eighth term.

J. Will Taylor (Republican, Tennessee) was in his tenth term when appointed to the Committee, and Carl Mapes (Republican, Michigan) and Hamilton Fish (Republican, New York) were commencing their eleventh terms. Adolph J. Sabath (Democrat, Illinois) was not appointed until his thirteenth. Ordinarily one would expect such

veterans to have accumulated so much seniority on another committee that they would not wish to assume a bottom rung on the Rules
Committee. Sabath, at the time of his move, was ranking member of
Immigration and Naturalization. Fish was ranking member of Foreign
Affairs and number two on Banking and Currency. He surrendered
the Banking and Currency position but was allowed to retain his place
on Foreign Affairs. Earl Michener (Republican, Michigan) kept the
number-three spot on Judiciary when he was assigned to Rules in his
fourth consecutive and eleventh nonconsecutive term.

Previous Committee Assignment. As Table 8 has shown, the first
requirement for assignment to the Rules Committee is usually considerable tenure as a Congressman. No generalization about previous
committee assignments can be so pat. During their several years
before going to Rules, members hold a variety of committee posts.
The presumption is that during one's first and second terms he may
expect assignment to a minor committee, e.g., Post Office and Civil
Service or District of Columbia.

One formula for measuring the prestige and importance of committees was devised by John C. Eberhart and was applied to all
committee assignments from 1914 to 1941. This formula included
length of service in the House when appointed, length of service on
the committee, the holding power of the committee, the drawing
power of the committee, and a combination of drawing and holding
powers. The results of Mr. Eberhart's calculations showed the thirteen most prestigious committees to be as follows:[6]

1. Ways and Means
2. Appropriations
3. Rules
4. Interstate and Foreign Commerce
5. Judiciary
6. Agriculture

[6] Reported in George B. Galloway, *Congress at the Crossroads* (New York:
Crowell, 1946), p. 90. For a recent study of assignments decisions, see
Nicholas A. Masters, "Committee Assignments in the House of Representa-
tives," *American Political Science Review,* 55 (1961), 345-57.

7. Foreign Affairs
8. Naval Affairs
9. Banking and Currency
10. Rivers and Harbors
11. Military Affairs
12. Post Office and Post Roads
13. Merchant Marine and Fisheries

A number of variables was omitted from this formula. For example, one would expect that the time of one's entering Congress might seriously affect his committee choice. Where young men have already stationed themselves and opportunities for rising to a chairmanship seem slight, one might prefer higher rank on a somewhat less prestigious committee. Nor should another variable be overlooked. One's constituency may have peculiar problems (aside from a member's own personal preferences) that make certain committee assignments more attractive than others. For example, an Oklahoma Democrat was pleased to leave Foreign Affairs for Interstate and Foreign Commerce because he believed the latter was more advantageous for his district. In short, Eberhart's formula is based on what members are able to get, not what they might like to get, and does not take into account the bases for a member's preference. Further, it was applied over a rather long period of time, and the prestige and importance of committees conceivably vary from time to time. For example, the Foreign Affairs Committee is believed to have increased in prestige in recent years as its role and the House's role in foreign policy have increased.[7] Nevertheless, for providing an overall view of Congressional evaluation of committees, Eberhart's findings are quite useful.

Given that Ways and Means and Appropriations rank ahead of Rules, one would predict that no member would leave either Ways and Means or Appropriations for an assignment on Rules. Between 1937-62 only Hamer Budge (Republican, Idaho) made such a move, but he was very near the bottom of the large Appropriations Com-

[7] Robert A. Dahl, *Congress and Foreign Policy* (New York: Harcourt, Brace, 1950), pp. 147-49, and Holbert N. Carroll, *The House of Representatives and Foreign Affairs* (Pittsburgh: University of Pittsburgh Press, 1958).

mittee. By going to the Rules Committee he became "low man," but with only three members ahead of him. On the other hand, Donald McClean (Republican, New Jersey) relinquished his place on the Rules Committee for a seat on Ways and Means. One would further predict that committees ranking just below Rules in prestige would be less likely to provide members for the Rules Committee than those farther down. In this case, one's prediction is not so neatly confirmed. As Table 9 shows, Interstate and Foreign Commerce, which ranked number four—just behind Rules—supplied seven members for Rules from 1937 to 1962; and Foreign Affairs, which ranked seventh, gave six members to Rules, although one of them, Hamilton Fish, retained his Foreign Affairs seat. Nor would one predict that members would leave the Rules Committee for an assignment on a committee with less prestige. Only Christian Herter (Republican, Massachusetts) resigned to go to a less prestigious committee, Foreign Affairs, where he could continue his professional interest in international relations. Joseph W. Martin and Charles Halleck (Republican, Indiana) both quit the Rules Committee to take more prestigious positions in the party's Congressional leadership.

Except for Foreign Affairs, Interstate and Foreign Commerce, and perhaps Banking and Currency, which supplied three members, prestigious committees lost very few members to Rules. On the other hand, most of the members came from committees with low prestige. Sabath gave up the ranking position on Immigration and Naturalization to move to Rules. J. Bayard Clark (Democrat, North Carolina) surrendered the chairmanship of an Elections Committee and Byron Harlan (Democrat, Ohio) resigned as chairman of the Committee on Revision of Laws to accept a place on Rules. William J. Driver (Democrat, Arkansas) and John E. Lyle (Democrat, Texas) did not find the number-two positions on Flood Control and Post Office and Civil Service sufficiently attractive to decline advancement to the Rules Committee. In 1961 Representative Carl Elliott (Democrat, Alabama) gave up a senior position and a "swing vote" on the Education and Labor Committee to move to Rules. The leadership wanted a "liberal," "pro-Administration" southerner who was also liked and respected throughout the House.

Table 9

PREVIOUS COMMITTEE ASSIGNMENTS OF MEMBERS OF COMMITTEE ON RULES, 1937-62

Interstate and Foreign Commerce	7
Foreign Affairs	6
Claims	5
Merchant Marine and Fisheries	5
Post Office and Civil Service	5
Accounts	4
Immigration and Naturalization	4
Military or Naval Affairs (later Armed Services)	4
Banking and Currency	3
District of Columbia	3
Elections	3
Expenditures in Executive Department	3
Insular Affairs	3
Judiciary	3
Public Buildings and Grounds	3
Territories	3
Veterans	3
Agriculture	2
Education and Labor	2
Flood Control	2
Rivers and Harbors	2
Appropriations	1
Census	1
Coinage, Weights and Measures	1
Home Administration	1
Immigration and Reclamation	1
Invalid Pensions	1
Mines and Minings	1
Patents	1
Public Lands	1
Public Works	1
Revision of Laws	1
Roads	1
Science and Aeronautical	1

With respect to previous committee assignment, one may say that the Rules Committee has been recruited from other committees with less prestige and that it has failed to attract important committee chairmen or other party leaders. Members may become formal or informal leaders after a tour of duty with Rules, as did Joseph Martin, Charles

Halleck, Leo Allen, Clarence Brown, Howard Smith, and Richard Bolling. But they are not put on the Committee as leaders.

CONSTITUENCY BACKGROUNDS

Membership by States. To what extent has the Committee been "representative" of the country? Criteria of representativeness are numerous and include states and regions as well as the competitive and urban characteristics of constituencies. As Table 10 shows, three

Table 10

DISTRIBUTION BY STATES OF MEMBERSHIP OF COMMITTEE ON RULES, 1937-62

1.	New York	7
2.	Indiana	4
3.	Massachusetts	4
4.	Illinois	3
5.	Missouri	3
6.	Ohio	3
7.	Texas	3
8.	Arkansas	2
9.	California	2
10.	Colorado	2
11.	Michigan	2
12.	Oklahoma	2
13.	Pennsylvania	2
14.	Tennessee	2
15.	Alabama	1
16.	Georgia	1
17.	Idaho	1
18.	Kansas	1
19.	Kentucky	1
20.	Mississippi	1
21.	New Jersey	1
22.	New Mexico	1
23.	North Carolina	1
24.	Oregon	1
25.	Virginia	1
26.	Washington	1
	TOTAL	53

states provided nearly one-third of the fifty-three members between 1937 and 1962. New York, Indiana, and Massachusetts supplied fifteen members whose total service amounted to sixty-four years, something just less than one-fifth the total man-years of membership from 1937 to 1962. Between 1951 and 1958 two neighboring New York districts were simultaneously represented by James J. Delaney (Democrat) and Henry J. Latham (Republican). One district, which embraces part of Kansas City, Missouri, has twice been represented on the Committee. Roger Slaughter (Democrat) served approximately three years before his opposition to President Truman, his best-known constituent, proved his undoing in the party primary. Richard Bolling (Democrat) came to Congress two years after Slaughter's defeat and moved to Rules six years later.

Regional Representation. Southern Democrats and midwestern Republicans have often been said to dominate the membership of the Committee. Table 11 classifies members by region both in absolute numbers and also in terms of years of service. Such a breakdown reveals that neither in numbers nor in years of service has the South monopolized the Committee. Its Democratic representatives account for about 23 per cent of the Committee's members and more than 30 per cent of the man-years of service, not to mention seven years served by two Tennessee Republicans. The Midwest contributed twelve members (from both parties) whose total service equalled 108 years. Thus, the South and Midwest occupied the Committee for 225 of the 334 years of service between 1937 and 1962. It is understandable why commentators have called the Committee a stronghold of southern Democrats and midwestern Republicans. At any one term the South will almost always possess half the complement of Democrats of the Committee, depending on the breadth of the term South.[8] During the term, 1939-1941, four of the nine Democrats were from the South. From 1955-60, the South claimed Smith

---

[8] The ratio of southern Democrats to all Democrats in the House between 1937 and 1952 varied from 30 per cent in 1937 to 46.8 per cent in 1943. Austin Ranney and Willmoore Kendall, *Democracy and the American Party System* (New York: Harcourt, Brace, 1956), p. 180.

Table 11

**REGIONAL DISTRIBUTION OF MEMBERSHIP
OF COMMITTEE ON RULES, 1937-62***

	In years of service	Number
DEMOCRATS		
East	30	4
South	110	10
Midwest	41	5
Border	21	5
West	6	3
REPUBLICANS		
East	36	10
South	7	2
Midwest	67	9
Border	2	1
West	14	4
BOTH PARTIES		
East	66	14
South	117	12
Midwest	108	14
Border	23	6
West	20	7
TOTAL	334	53

* Regional strength can vary according to one's definitions of regions. In this case the following definitions were employed based largely on conventional usage as illustrated by V. O. Key, *Southern Politics* (New York: Alfred A. Knopf, 1950) and John Fenton, *Politics in the Border States* (New Orleans: The Hauser Press, 1957); Duncan MacRae, Jr., *Dimensions of Congressional Voting* (Berkeley: University of California Press, 1958):
East: Mass., N. J., N. Y., Pa.
South: Ala., Ark., Ga., Miss., N. C., Tenn., Tex., Va.
Midwest: Ill., Ind., Kans., Mich., Ohio.
Border: Ky., Mo., Okla.
West: Calif., Colo., Idaho, N. Mex., Ore., Wash.

(Virginia), Colmer (Mississippi), Trimble (Arkansas), and Thornberry (Texas), or half the Democratic side of the table; and when two Democrats were added in 1961, one was a southerner (Elliott, Alabama).

The East has contributed more members than any other section, but the rapid turnover among New England and Middle Atlantic Congressmen makes for a comparatively small number of years of service. The West unquestionably has enjoyed very little direct representation. The California Democratic delegation expressed feelings

of hurt pride when it asked for a Western member in 1945.[9] At
that time, only one Committee member was from west of the Mississippi River and none came from west of the Missouri River. In 1959
the Republicans appointed Hamer Budge (Idaho), but he was defeated in the general election of 1960. When the House enlarged the
Committee in 1961, the Democrats added B. J. Sisk and the Republicans chose H. Allen Smith (both of California).

Thus, the South and Midwest have been at an advantage and the
West at a decided disadvantage in obtaining places on the Rules Committee. The East and Border States have done reasonably well in
earning assignments, but they have been unable to retain them for
seniority purposes.

Urban vs. Rural Representation. Table 12 confirms the frequent
observation that rural districts are more often represented on the
Committee than urban constituencies. Both parties have chosen their
members predominantly from among rural Congressmen, but the

Table 12

**URBAN — RURAL DISTRIBUTION OF MEMBERS
OF RULES COMMITTEE, 1937-62***

Number of Members from Urban Districts		21
Republicans	8	
Democrats	13	
Number of Members from Rural Districts		32
Republicans	18	
Democrats	14	
TOTAL		53
Man-Years of Service by Members from Urban Districts		117
Republicans	31	
Democrats	86	
Man-Years of Service by Members from Rural Districts		217
Republicans	95	
Democrats	122	
TOTAL		334

* Rural districts were designated as those which included four or more counties,
unless a large metropolitan area obviously dominated several outlying counties.

[9] Floyd M. Riddick, "The First Session of the Seventy-Ninth Congress,"
American Political Science Review, 45 (1946), 263.

Republicans have been even more inclined to appoint country representatives. The rural advantage is illustrated not only by the number of terms of members from urban or rural areas, but also by the number of *man-years of service* by city and country Congressmen. Whereas slightly more than 60 per cent of the appointments has been rural, nearly 65 per cent of the man-years of service has also been rural.

Safe and Competitive Districts. It is often said in the House that some legislators welcome a committee of members from safe districts who are willing and able to resist pressures for certain classes of legislation. An examination of the constituencies that sent members to the Rules Committee from 1937 to 1962 shows a decidedly favorable representation of safe districts. As shown in Table 13, thirty-seven

Table 13

SAFE — COMPETITIVE CHARACTER OF CONSTITUENCIES OF MEMBERS OF COMMITTEE ON RULES, 1937-62*

In numbers

Safe		37
Republican	19	
Democratic	18	
Competitive		16
Republican	6	
Democratic	10	
TOTAL		53

In man-years of service

Safe		270
Republican	104	
Democratic	166	
Competitive		64
Republican	22	
Democratic	42	
TOTAL		334

* An extensive discussion, including citations of the relevant literature, of problems of operationalizing concepts of safeness and competitiveness is contained in William H. Standing and James A. Robinson, "Inter-Party Competition and Primary Contesting," *American Political Science Review*, 52 (1958), 1066-77.

(70 per cent) of the fifty-three members came from districts in which re-election was hardly in doubt, and these men accumulated 270 (84 per cent) of the 334 man-years of service during the twenty-six-year period. The sixteen representatives from competitive election jurisdictions accounted for only sixty-four man-years.

CONSEQUENCES FOR POLICY

What are the consequences for public policy of the organizational experience and constituencies represented on the Rules Committee? Does it make any difference for the Committee's decisions that most of its members have had three or four terms of service on lesser committees, and that a majority are from safe, rural districts of the South and Midwest?

The implications of selecting third and fourth termers from minor committees mainly relate to finding men who are in harmony with their party leaderships. The apprenticeship period allows party leaders to observe the talents and temperaments of new members for working within the established patterns of Congressional activity. For such a role, the public's image of a Congressman matters little. What counts is how his organizational peers evaluate him. The leadership wants men who will "go along" when a party issue is at stake and who can "take the heat" for the House. The apprenticeship trains men in these respects and allows the leaders to identify those suited for a place on the Committee.

That the leadership is concerned about this kind of party regularity is well illustrated in Speaker Rayburn's correspondence of November and December, 1948. The elections restored the Democrats to majority status after two years as the minority party. This automatically created four new positions on the Rules Committee, and the death of John Delaney (New York) created a fifth vacancy. Within hours after the election, colleagues were wiring or writing Speaker Rayburn at his home in Bonham, Texas, about the composition of the Committee. Rayburn promised Chairman Sabath, "I will see what can be done about not loading you down with people who will not work with the Democrats."[10] To John McCormack he mentioned two southerners as possible new Committee members and thought that the East, North, and West should have "three loyal Democrats" appointed.[11] And the senior Democrat (Jere Cooper, Tennessee) on the Ways and Means Committee, which is the Democratic Committee on Committees, wrote the Speaker about a number of young members whom he and others had been watching for possible promotion to major committees. Several of those he mentioned distinguished themselves sooner or later in national politics—Hart of New Jersey, Feighan of Ohio, Kennedy of Massachusetts, Mansfield of Montana, Karsten of Missouri, Blatnik of Minnesota, Stigler of Oklahoma, Hedrich of West Virginia, Dr. Morgan of Pennsylvania, and Buchanan of Pennsylvania.[12] The emphasis was on reliability and regularity as observed during the apprenticeship.

How might one demonstrate that the apprenticeship *actually* serves these functions? Assuming that the leadership tries to pick members who "go along," one can expect it to choose men who more often than not vote with the majority of their party against the majority of the opposition party. There may be as many as fifty or sixty such opportunities each Congress. The *Congressional Quarterly* annually computes and publishes a "party unity" score for every member, based on the roll-call votes, which divide the majority of one party against the majority of the other. The party unity score is actually the percentage of votes on which the member sides with the majority of his own party. If assumptions about the leadership's criteria for choosing Rules Committee members are correct, one expects new members to have high party unity scores prior to their assignment to the Committee. Table 14 shows the data for thirty-two cases for which the party unity scores are available in terms prior to appointment. All but one of the Democrats had scores of 80 per cent or higher. The

[10] Rayburn to Sabath, November 15, 1948, Rayburn Papers, Rayburn Library, 1948 files, Miscellaneous A-2, July–December.

[11] Rayburn to McCormack, December 9, 1948, *ibid*.

[12] Cooper to Rayburn, November 19, 1948, *ibid*.

Table 14

PARTY UNITY SCORES OF TERM PRIOR TO APPOINTMENT, 1945-61*

PARTY UNITY SCORE	*Democrats*	*Republicans*	*Total*
90-100	6	8	14
80-89	6	4	10
70-79	1	3	4
60-69	0	2	2
50-59	0	1	1
40-49	0	1	1
TOTAL	13	19	32

* "Term prior to appointment" is the term immediately preceding appointment. In the cases of members who were not in Congress in the immediately preceding period, their scores are for the last term they served before their membership lapsed. Members who were temporarily dislodged as a result of alteration in party control of the House are counted again when they are returned to the Committee. Thus, the 32 cases actually are based on 28 individuals.

exception was William Colmer (79 per cent), who was *reappointed* in 1949 on the basis of prior membership and not because the leadership regarded him as cooperative. Actually, Speaker Rayburn would have preferred to drop Colmer because "we just cannot depend on him in the pinches,"[13] but Colmer received promise of support from John McCormack before Rayburn could pass the word to the Majority Leader. Three-fourths of the Republicans also had scores higher than 80 per cent.

The fact that so many Committee members are from safe districts is often thought to have the effects of reducing the temptations to follow particular constituent interests and of raising the probability of the Committee's taking a party or a national position. One midwestern Democrat, in applying to Speaker Rayburn for membership, cited his large majorities and the likelihood of his continuing to have a safe seat.[14] On the other hand, it is also often asserted that Congressmen who must worry about re-election will be more sensitive to the "will of the people," whatever that may be and however it may be calculated.

Does it make any difference for public policy that safe districts are

[13] Rayburn to Cooper, November 22, 1948, *ibid.*
[14] Ray Madden to Rayburn, November, 1948, *ibid.*

represented much more heavily than competitive districts? The easiest way to answer this question is to compare the party unity scores of these two classifications of Committee. These data are available for thirty-eight members who served 110 terms (or 220 man-years) between the 79th (1945-46) and 87th Congresses (1961-62). The overwhelming number of terms (ninety-two) served by safe members as compared with terms (eighteen) served by competitive members leaves a rather small number of competitive terms of service. However, as Table 15 shows, the members most inclined to have low party

Table 15

PARTY UNITY SCORES OF SAFE AND COMPETITIVE MEMBERS, 1945-62

PARTY UNITY SCORE	SAFE	*Percentage*	COMPETITIVE	*Percentage*
90-100	32	*34.8*	5	*27.7*
80-89	23	*25.0*	4	*22.2*
70-79	12	*13.0*	7	*38.9*
60-69	8	*8.7*	0	*0.0*
50-59	6	*6.5*	0	*0.0*
40-49	8	*8.7*	2	*11.1*
30-39	3	*3.3*	0	*0.0*
20-29	1	*1.1*	0	*0.0*
TOTAL	92	*101.1*	18	*99.9*

unity scores are from safe districts. That is, most of the Committeemen whose roll-call voting is against the majority of their own party are members who ordinarily can count on re-election. Although the number of terms held by representatives of competitive districts is small, only two were served by men who voted with their party less than 60 per cent of the time.

What about differences in roll-call voting between urban and rural members? Table 16 shows that a higher proportion of urban members voted with their party than rural. In other words, rural members seem more inclined to depart from their party's central position and side with the opposition. The proposition is further strengthened by looking more specifically at the only two urban representatives whose party

Table 16

PARTY UNITY SCORES OF URBAN AND RURAL MEMBERS, 1945-62

PARTY UNITY SCORES	URBAN	*Percentage*	RURAL	*Percentage*
90-100	19	*43.2*	18	*26.7*
80-89	13	*29.5*	14	*20.9*
70-79	10	*22.9*	9	*13.4*
60-69	0	*0.0*	8	*11.9*
50-59	0	*0.0*	6	*8.9*
40-49	2	*4.5*	8	*11.9*
30-39	0	*0.0*	3	*4.4*
20-29	0	*0.0*	1	*1.5*
TOTAL	44	*100.1*	67	*99.6*

unity scores were below 70 per cent. Both were Republicans from competitive districts, and their tendency to join Democrats on roll calls was probably motivated by their need for electoral survival. In dissenting they moved closer to the House norm.

So far party regularity has been used as an index of policy or decision preference, and factors have been sought in constituency backgrounds on which policy position might depend. However, as students of roll-call analysis delight in pointing out, partisan roll calls represent only part of Congressional activity. They are the top of the iceberg, as it were. On many socially significant roll calls, i.e., on bills with wide scope and important domains, the majorities of each party agree and combine to defeat minorities within both parties. *Congressional Quarterly* also computes a "Bipartisan Unity" score, which will help to determine whether safe and competitive and urban and rural members differ in their support of bipartisan House majorities. (This analysis is also relevant to the discussion in Chapter 4, which emphasized the norm that the Committee try to represent House majorities as well as strictly party positions.)

Data are available for the 83rd (1953-54) through the 86th Congresses (1959-60) for nineteen individuals or a total of forty-eight cases and are displayed in Table 17. They suggest several important generalizations. First, the small number of competitive cases of bipartisan scores makes comparison of safe and competitive performance

Table 17

BIPARTISAN UNITY SCORES AND COMPETITIVENESS AND URBANISM OF MEMBERS' CONSTITUENCIES, 1953-60

SCORE	SAFE	*Percentage*	COMPETITIVE	*Percentage*	URBAN	*Percentage*	RURAL	*Percentage*
90-100	5	*13.1*	3	*30*	3	*15*	5	*17.8*
80-89	8	*21.0*	3	*30*	8	*40*	3	*10.7*
70-79	13	*34.2*	2	*20*	7	*35*	8	*28.5*
60-69	7	*18.4*	2	*20*	2	*10*	7	*25.0*
Below 60	5	*13.1*	0	*00*	0	*0*	5	*17.8*
TOTAL	38	*99.8*	10	*100*	20	*100*	28	*99.8*

difficult; however, members from competitive constituencies tend to vote with the House majority more often than members from safe districts. Second, urban members are more likely to be with the bipartisan majority than rural members, and the latter are more likely to be among the House minority. These two findings add further evidence to the view that safe and rural constituencies allow the members to isolate themselves from colleagues who compose majorities.

Third, the data raise some question about the Committee's being representative of the House majority. It will be recalled that one of the rationalizations for a member's departing from the majority party's demands is in order to represent the majority of the House. But Table 17 shows that, frequently, Rules Committeemen differ from the House majority when bills reach the roll-call stage on the House floor.

One caveat must be entered to this analysis. Roll-call votes on the House floor may be different from votes in the Rules Committee. Some members occasionally vote to report a bill but reserve the right to vote against it on the floor. The frequency of this "divided vote" is not known, but its existence is well known. Trimble and Thornberry, for example, have on occasion voted to report civil rights bills that they later voted against on final passage in the House.

In short, there appear to be considerable policy differences between safe and competitive members and between members from rural and urban areas. Within the Committee these differences can be surmounted and a rule granted when the issue is salient enough to bring the House leadership's pressure to bear, but it is not so vital to the member's own constituency that he must choose between House and constituency interests. On the other hand, when the leadership's and House's interests are unknown or unexpressed, the values of rural, southern, midwestern, and safe constituencies have an advantage in the Committee.

6

Proposed Reforms:
Party Responsibility
versus
Legislative Independence

THE LEGISLATIVE
Reorganization Act of 1946 left three controversial Congressional procedures untouched. These were the seniority system in both Houses,[1] the filibuster in the Senate,[2] and the Rules Committee in the House. About the seniority system no realistic person expects to do anything. Most legislators, and many observers, conclude that, with all its faults, the merits are greater. But about the filibuster and the Rules Committee, there are periodic efforts toward change. This concluding chapter evaluates proposals to reform the Rules Committee in light of two different normative theories of Congressional politics.

The first is the doctrine of party responsibility.[3] This theory of party government assumes that alternative parties ought to present clear-cut programs to the electorate, and that the victorious party should be held responsible at subsequent elections for the enactment and enforcement of its campaign promises. The modern British sys-

[1] George Goodwin, Jr., "The Seniority System in Congress," *American Political Science Review*, 53 (1959), 412-36.

[2] Franklin L. Burdette, *Filibustering in the Senate* (Princeton: Princeton University Press, 1940).

[3] For a lucid and interesting explication of the origins and implications of this idea, see Austin Ranney, *The Doctrine of Responsible Party Government* (Urbana: University of Illinois Press, 1954, 1962).

tem is often taken as a descriptive model of what a responsible party system should be like.

The second normative doctrine postulates the need for independence—even some competition—between the legislative and executive branches, from which emerges a system of checks and balances.[4] This second theory stresses Congress as an institution, whereas the first would develop political parties into more organized governing institutions. The theory based on legislative independence postulates a process of *bargaining,* in which Congressional leaders check, balance, and control executive leaders, whereas the party responsibility doctrine postulates a *polyarchal* process in which nonleaders (the electorate) control both Congressional and executive leaders through responsible parties.[5] Legislative independence would make Congress, in the form of a bipartisan institution, a check on the presidency. Party responsibility would promote parties in competition at the expense of bipartisan alignments and would rely on Republican-Democratic competition to check the government (both Congress and President) organized by one party only.

The accompanying diagram displays the nature of the competitive process preferred by these alternative doctrines, in terms of a Democratic majority party.

Party Responsibility	*Legislative Independence*
Democrats (both Presidential and Congressional)	Congress (both Democrats and Republicans)
vs.	vs.
Republicans (both Congressional and aspiring Presidential candidates)	President (Democrat)

[4] For a statement of this point of view, see Charles S. Hyneman, *Bureaucracy in a Democracy* (New York: Harper and Row, 1950), esp. pp. 38-74.

[5] The terms bargaining and polyarchy are used here as in Robert A. Dahl and Charles E. Lindblom, *Politics, Economics, Welfare* (New York: Harper and Row, 1953).

Before considering the speech proposals to promote party responsibility or legislative independence, we must first consider a procedural obstacle to any kind of reform.

PROCEDURAL OBSTACLE TO REFORM

All proposed reforms confront the same obstacle: the Rules Committee has jurisdiction over resolutions to change the *Rules* of the House, and, therefore, has jurisdiction over proposals to alter its own formal powers. It is unlikely that the Committee would report a resolution designed to reduce its authority in the policy-making process, although in 1961 the Democratic caucus instructed the Committee to report a resolution to enlarge its membership to fifteen. If the Committee were so co-operative as to report willingly a resolution curbing its power, there would hardly be any need for basic reforms.

However, there are two means of by-passing this bottleneck. One is the Discharge Petition. If a majority of House members (218) care enough to reform the Committee, they can discharge it of any resolution and on the appropriate day call up and pass the resolution. A second means of circumventing the Committee's stranglehold on the House *Rules* is the strategy adopted at the first sittings of the 81st, 82nd, and 88th Congresses. The majority amended the *Rules* pertaining to the Committee at the time of the traditional motion to readopt the *Rules* of the previous Congress. This motion is not referred to Committee but is settled promptly by the House.

There is, in short, no real and insurmountable parliamentary obstacle to reforming the Rules Committee, providing the necessary votes are available. The failure of reform moves in the past cannot be explained wholly by complicated parliamentary situations. The three close votes on the 21-Day Rule and the even closer vote to increase the size in 1961 testify to the continuing doubt the House has about its preferences.

REFORMS TO PROMOTE PARTY RESPONSIBILITY

After World War II the American Political Science Association received reports from three committees created to evaluate certain political institutions and to suggest reforms. One of these dealt with Congress, another with political parties, and a third with state legislatures.[6] The report from the Committee on Political Parties drew more attention and discussion than that of either of the other committees, but the document on Congress appeared about the time of the debate on legislative reorganization and perhaps had more influence on political practice.

It is a thin paper, which represents neither its authors nor the profession at their best. Excluding the preface and appendices, the report consisted of seventy-two pages. One can count only ten pages that might conceivably be regarded as descriptive or analytic. The rest are devoted to suggesting reforms with only unsupported assertions about why Congress needs reforming. No attempt is made to fulfill the slightest burden of proving the need for a better Congress or convincingly demonstrating particular shortcomings in Congressional procedure. No criteria are proffered by which either laymen, political scientists, or politicians might evaluate Congress or the proposed reforms.

The preface states,

> We have considered it to be our function not to undertake further research since the legislative field has already been extensively explored, but to study and discuss the problems of Congress much as the Rules Committees of that body might and sometimes do, holding

[6] *The Reorganization of Congress: A Report of the Committee on Congress of the American Political Science Association* (Washington: Public Affairs Press, 1945); "Toward a More Responsible Two-Party System," *American Political Science Review,* 44 (1950), supplement; Belle Zeller, editor, *American State Legislatures: Report of the Committee on American Legislatures, American Political Science Association* (New York: Thomas Y. Crowell Company, 1954).

hearings from time to time and inviting interested legislators to present their views.[7]

This limitation on the Committee's assignment was surely reasonable enough, but one looks in vain for evidence from the extensive exploration, to which the preface alludes, to support alleged needs of reform. As an example of a proposed change in party and Congressional practice, which is accompanied by not a single word of justification, consider the following sentence, which comes at the end of a descriptive paragraph (one of the few such paragraphs in the report) about the selection of committee members: "No change is proposed in the method of selecting committee members except to call attention to a logical suggestion that the Democrats in the House follow the Republican practice and set up a separate Committee on Committees instead of using a legislative committee (Ways and Means) for this purpose."[8] Just why this suggestion is "logical" the reader is not told, nor is there any indication of what different results would be expected from a change in the composition of the Democratic Committee on Committees.

The Report does not consider the Rules Committee directly. Whether it should be abolished or merely have its authority sharply reduced is not clear. The Report proposes that a Legislative Council be established "to plan and co-ordinate the legislative program of Congress and to promote more effective liaison and co-operation with the Executive."[9] This Council would include the Vice-President, Speaker, Majority Leader, and chairmen of recognized standing com-

[7] *The Reorganization of Congress*, p. 4.

[8] *Ibid.*, pp. 33-34.

[9] *Ibid.*, p. 79. Several similar proposals for a Legislative Cabinet or Central Council also have been advanced. Roland Young once urged reducing the number of committees in each House to nine, electing the chairmen by party caucus, and authorizing them to determine the content of legislation to be debated on the floor and the timing of consideration in hearings and on the floor. *This is Congress* (New York: Alfred A. Knopf, 1946, second edition), p. 248. Charles S. Hyneman has proposed a Central Council consisting of legislative leaders meeting frequently with the President in order to control the bureaucracy and see that it administers law as Congress intended (*Bureaucracy in a Democracy*, Chap. 25).

mittees. The extent to which the Speaker, the Majority Leader, and committee chairmen would "plan and co-ordinate" the business of the House is not detailed.

In a recent monograph, Dr. George Galloway, one of the foremost writers on Congress, cites "three serious defects that handicap its [the Rules Committee's] performance as a majority policy committee."[10] First, the Committee is not truly representative of the majority party of the House. As seen in Chapter 5, there is skewed distribution of seats among the states and regions.

Galloway would like the Rules Committee to serve as a majority policy committee, not as an agent of the House, and he regards regional representation and selection as a significant correlate of a member's voting behavior. He endorses the proposals of Dr. Lewis J. Lapham to elect the committee geographically.

Galloway's second criticism of the Rules Committee as a majority policy committee is that some of its members are from the minority. In 1884 Woodrow Wilson made this same criticism of all Congressional committees.[11] Within the context of the doctrine of party responsibility, there is a certain logic to making the majority party assume sole responsibility for legislation. But in the twentieth century the Congressional conception of relations between political parties has not been one that allows the majority of the majority party to have its way, to do all the work, and to treat the minority as mere observers who happen to be seated on the floor instead of in the galleries. Congress divides all its work, including investigations, hearings, and program-arranging among members of both parties and encourages the minority leaders to participate in planning the program of the House.

Robert Luce, first a member of the Massachusetts legislature and then for many terms in the House of Representatives, commented on this trait of Congressional practice in one of his several books on legislation.

[10] *Congress and Parliament: Their Organization and Operation in the U. S. and U. K.* (Washington: National Planning Association, 1955), p. 37.

[11] *Congressional Government,* p. 81.

Our system does give the opportunity for many minds to help. Every member of Congress has the chance to contribute toward good legislation. If he belongs to the majority party, he is not necessarily a voting dummy as in Parliament; if he belongs to the minority, he is not restricted to mere faultfinding, as Mr. Wilson wanted him to be, but in the committee room may play a most useful part in constructive effort for the public good. It should always be remembered that anyhow only a few big questions, if any, call for aggressive political leadership. The great mass of the business of every legislative body is nonpartisan in nature.[12]

The same logic that justifies excluding the minority representatives from the Rules Committee justifies excluding them from other committees. But to put all the "responsibility" on the majority members would reduce the number of people among whom the work can be shared. Whether Congress would produce better legislation and be more "responsible" to the wishes and interests of the country must be left to speculation.

Galloway's third criticism is closely related to his second, and, indeed, would be eliminated if the membership of the Rules Committee were limited to the majority party. He cites the southern Democratic-Republican coalition on the Committee as an impediment to the accomplishment of the majority's program. There have been, as earlier portions of this book revealed, instances in which a bipartisan alliance dominated the Committee. It was to circumvent this obstacle that the 21-Day Rule was designed. But the fact that that Rule was repealed, that few special orders have been discharged, and that few rules have been defeated by the House would seem to indicate that the bipartisan coalition often reflects the philosophy of the House. If one desires that the Rules Committee act as agent of the House, he presumably has much to be satisfied about in looking at its record over the last twenty years.

If one desires a Rules Committee to act as agent of the majority party, he may not be so satisfied. However, given the apparent differ-

---

[12] *Congress, An Explanation* (Cambridge: Harvard University Press, 1926), p. 107.

ences of philosophy within a party whose representatives come from districts differing widely in many respects, it is questionable whether there is a stable majority within a majority party. To ask a Democrat from Maine to adhere to the same party line as a Democrat from Arkansas may mean that the Democratic party in Congress will have one less member after the next election. If the party's electoral system is not strictly responsible—i.e., one that will produce candidates of relatively similar philosophies so that voters may be certain to distinguish Democrat from Republican—one seems justified in speculating whether Congress ought to be organized along altogether different conceptions of responsibility.

Nevertheless, the theory of responsible parties spawns other reform ideas. Dr. Lewis J. Lapham, whose suggestions for reform have been given currency in Dr. Galloway's publications,[13] closed his doctoral dissertation with several proposals for changing the selection process of the Committee.[14] Lapham's objective is unequivocal. He too prefers such an organization of the parties and the House that the onus of blame or the praise of credit may be placed on the parties who in fact make the decisions. At present, responsibility is dispersed among the leadership, the committee chairmen, and the Rules Committee. No single person or policy committee can speak for all these little potentates; or, if there were such a leader or group of leaders, they could not promise to mobilize and deliver the overwhelming vote of their party.

Lapham is disturbed by the under-representation of some parts of the country and by the fact that members who acquire stations on the Committee in one generation hold them for another generation, not because they are in harmony with the will of the party, but because of seniority. He, therefore, proposes the following corrective measures:

[13] *Congress and Parliament,* p. 38.

[14] *Party Leadership and the House Committee on Rules* (Ph.D. thesis, Harvard University, 1953), pp. 360-74. Some similar, although less numerous and not so fully developed, reforms are advocated by Christopher Van Hollen, *The House Committee on Rules (1933-1951): Agent of Party and Agent of Opposition* (Ph.D. dissertation, The Johns Hopkins University, 1951), pp. 291-99.

(1) that for the purpose of selecting this Committee the country be divided into eight regions and that each region be entitled to at least one and not more than three members according to party strength; (2) that the majority party caucus elect members of the Committee; (3) that the number of members be raised to sixteen; (4) that the minority be excluded from voting membership, although it might send six or eight observers who presumably would act as the Rules Committee if election returns were reversed; (5) that the Committee elect its own chairman. Proposals one and four were mentioned in discussing Galloway's criticisms of the Committee. Only parts two, three, and five of Lapham's suggestions will be treated here.

First, consider the suggestion that members of this Committee be *elected by the majority party caucus.* Formally speaking, this is the way members are now chosen. Lapham would reconstitute the Committee at the beginning of each Congress rather than follow the seniority rule by which a member is automatically reappointed. The intent of periodic election is to remove assurances of continued tenure if the member does not fulfill the wishes of the majority. Hence, responsible party government is promoted.

Whether Lapham's proposal would produce what he prefers is questionable. At present, nominations to the Committee must be confirmed by the party caucus. The nominations are made by the Committee on Committees at the suggestion of the leadership. There is no reason to think that the nominating committees will be any less decisive in structuring the decision of the caucus under Lapham's plan than under present procedures.

However, perhaps if the whole committee had to be re-elected each year (as in theory it is now), and if it were understood (as it is *not* now) that the seniority rule were not to apply, the caucus would show greater activity. Such elections would seem to be rather similar to those that each party now conducts for Speaker, Leader, and Whip. Yet these contests take place only when there is a vacancy; after a post is once filled, the same member is likely to occupy it until he voluntarily relinquishes it. One is uncertain whether such changes would increase the Committee's sense of responsibility.

On the subject of responsibility Lapham does not always maintain his usual clarity. He proposes to choose the Committee in caucus, but later he says that his method of selection will make the Committee the strong arm of the leadership. Now, if the leadership continues to propose members and the caucus automatically confirms them, Lapham need not worry about the Committeemen ever doubting to whom they are responsible. Clearly they will be aware that they got their posts through the good offices of the leadership. On the other hand, if the caucus actively participates in the selection, one may have cause to wonder whether it is going to produce a strong arm for the leadership. If one believes region to be important in attitudes and voting, it is not too farfetched to conceive that one geographic section, the South for example, might be at odds with the leadership on an issue; and if this issue were the most important one to the region, it might select its representatives for the Committee according to their views on that issue. Further, if the leadership does not make the nominations, the sections will propose names that the House is likely to accept in virtually all cases. It is difficult to conceive of the caucus defeating the three names proposed by the South. Such a method would contribute to further sectionalism and bargaining between regions rather than to making a party or a Congress with "a national point of view."

Lapham also suggests *enlarging the Committee to sixteen members*. With all sixteen from one party the various groups might be more accurately represented, which is the intention of the proposal. However, the House is not likely to be sampled more precisely by sixteen than by twelve or fifteen, the usual size of the Committee. In the past, the size of the Committee has varied with attempts of various forces to control it; there is no magic in the number per se.

Finally, Dr. Lapham proposes that the Committee *elect its own chairman* rather than be presided over by the member whose consecutive years of service on the Committee are most numerous. How much difference this would make in the Committee's performance is open to speculation. Adolph Sabath (Democrat, Illinois) was Chairman from 1939 to 1952 and was frequently in the minority on vital issues of policy. His experience illustrates that the Chairman cannot obstruct a majority on the Committee. The case of Howard W. Smith (Democrat, Virginia), the present Chairman, further illustrates the same point. Smith is one of the most conservative and independent members of the House (as his party unity score compiled by *Congressional Quarterly* reveals). He is often in the minority as the Committee is now constituted. Although he can delay holding a hearing on a controversial bill, he cannot delay action indefinitely, if a Committee majority takes any initiative. When the majority wishes, it can force him to hear a request. Chairmen are permitted the initiative in arranging the Committee's work, but this is by custom, not by explicit House *Rules*.

REFORMS TO PROMOTE LEGISLATIVE INDEPENDENCE

Among proposals to strengthen Congress vis-à-vis the presidency is that of former Dean W. Reed West of The George Washington University, who urged the Joint Committee on the Reorganization of Congress to restore the Speaker to the Rules Committee. Dean West, a political scientist with conservative party politics,[15] contends that Congress needs to be encouraged to resume "the initiative in the formulation of policy," which requires the "establishment of a responsible leadership." Dean West contends that "it is ridiculous that the man who, more than any other person, has the confidence of the House, is barred from serving on the Committee that has most to do with the over-all control of the business of the House."[16] He proposed putting the floor leaders of both parties, as well as the Speaker, on the Committee. It will be recalled that the Speaker was prohibited from serving on this Committee when the Insurgents dethroned Cannon in

[15] See his article in a debate with Arthur M. Schlesinger, Jr., "Senator Taft's Foreign Policy," *Atlantic*, CLXXXIX, number 6 (June, 1952), 50-52.

[16] *Hearings before the Joint Committee on the Organization of Congress, 79th Congress, First Session* (Washington: Government Printing Office, 1945), pp. 1020-23.

1910. The Legislative Reorganization Act removed this prohibition, but did not go so far as Dean West and encourage the Speaker to return to the Committee.

West also proposed that each party form a genuine policy committee to consist of the Speaker, Rules Committee members, and several other members elected by the party caucus without reference to seniority. This committee would plan the legislative program and give leadership to its enactment. How this committee would affect the Rules Committee was not considered in West's testimony. One of two possibilities would seem likely. If the Rules Committee became subordinate to the policy committee, West's objective of strengthening the Congressional position against the executive branch would probably be served. But if, on the other hand, the Rules Committee asserted its independence of the policy committee, West's proposal contains no formal authority for the policy committee to discipline or overrule the Rules Committee. Whether more "responsible leadership" would be the result of such reforms remains speculative.

There is a further proposal to provide the Committee with a small research staff. The purpose of such assistance would be to survey the bills reported by legislative committees and to prepare the Committee on those for which hearings have been requested. This kind of assistance would no doubt help the Committee determine the cost of bills and aid it in reviewing the work of other committees. If not completely an instrument of the Chairman, it could share information more widely among all members of the Committee. However, the Committee's role in policy-making probably would increase at the expense of the doctrine that the Committee should merely help with arranging the House program. A staff of qualified researchers would be likely to take the initiative to inform members of the Committee about policy matters and to structure and determine the attention of the Committee.

Another possible change is in the procedure for handling Congressional differences in the same bill. It does not seem reasonable that unanimous consent be required to send to conference a bill that has already passed the House. Nor does it seem necessary to involve the Rules Committee at all. There is no apparent reason why motions to request a conference with the Senate could not be privileged (conference reports *after* House-Senate agreements are privileged now) and subject to a majority vote. Amendments to the motion providing instructions to the conferees could be in order. Such a change would strengthen the corporate position of Congress as a whole and leave it less subject to minority vetoes.

Some have suggested reducing the number of signatures required to discharge the Rules Committee. At present 218 members must sign a petition to take a bill from the Committee and bring it to the floor. Even when a majority favors a bill locked in the Committee, its members may not feel strongly enough to sign the petition for fear that, if the practice becomes a habit, their own committees may be similarly discharged. However, there is nothing sacred about the number 218. Until the Democratic majority swelled with New Deal election victories, the number was 145; before that, 100. The requisite number has altered to protect the majority party from embarrassment by the minority or by a hardy band of defectors from the majority.

The most revolutionary proposal, however, has not been seriously considered, and that is to eliminate altogether the Rules Committee's participation in decisions affecting the House agenda. Galloway comes close in suggesting that the minority party not be represented on the Committee. Most Congressmen assume that if there were no Rules Committee, one would have to be invented. They are partly right; someone or some group would need to be responsible for determining what committee bills should be considered, in what order, for how long, and whether they should be open for amendment. In the American state legislatures a wide variety of practices is available to perform these functions.[17]

And in the U. S. House of Representatives, these functions *could* be performed by someone other than the Rules Committee. Why not

[17] *American State Legislatures,* pp. 192-99; John C. Wahlke, Heinz Eulau, William Buchanan, and Leroy C. Ferguson, *The Legislative System: Explorations in Legislative Behavior* (New York: John Wiley and Sons, Inc., 1962), pp. 52-66.

"What's This Ugly Talk About Applying Rules to ME?"
—*Herblock in The Washington Post.*

the majority party leadership? As of now the leadership shares these responsibilities: after the Rules Committee grants a rule the Speaker and Majority Leader decide when to call it up, and when the rule is adopted the leadership determines when to debate the bill. Why not, then, leave it to the Speaker to recognize the Majority Leader to offer a privileged motion that the House consider a bill reported by a committee, under certain conditions governing time and amendments?

Such a motion would not be dissimilar to the present procedure, and it could, as is now the case, be subject to an hour's debate, divided equally between the Majority and Minority Leaders, and a majority of those present and voting would be required for its adoption. Amendments could be offered either to lengthen debate or to give special consideration to an alternative form of the bill.

The traditions of the House are hallowed with majority leaders' respect for minority leaders, and it is inconceivable that the majority party would discontinue the long-standing practice of consulting with the opposition party in scheduling items for debate and vote. In the event the majority leadership delay or deny calling up a bill, any member could offer a similar privileged motion. This is unlikely to happen, unless the leadership is clearly frustrating the majority. If it is not, it can easily defeat any such motion.

Although it is a smaller body, the Senate formerly determined its agenda by majority vote, usually on motion of the Majority Leader. In recent years it has gone even further in the direction of central leadership. Upon the recommendation of the Majority Leader, after consultation with opposition leaders and committee chairmen, the Senate sets its agenda by unanimous consent agreements. If a group of one hundred men can agree unanimously on its legislative program, four hundred men can surely operate by majority vote.

The mechanisms of this alternative are virtually the same as going through the Rules Committee, but the difference is that agenda-making decisions are centralized in the majority party leadership. These men have wider "reference groups" than the Rules Committee; they must work with all elements of their party, indeed with most elements of the House. The Speaker is a national official—after the Vice-

President he is first in succession to a vacant presidency. He and the Majority Leader participate in legislative conferences at the White House. In short, their public is larger than a single Congressional district. Although the national interest is an elusive object to identify, these leaders are more likely to consider wider interests than is the Rules Committee.

The Rules Committee would be retained to preside over basic questions of House procedure. As in the Senate, it could eventually be combined with the Administration Committee, which handles personnel and equipment. The Committee could or could not continue to have authority to report rules making in order bills that have not yet been acted on in other committees—an authority it rarely uses—but by either alternative, it would no longer possess a potential veto over bills already reported.

One of the major effects of this extensive change would be to concentrate additional power in the majority party leadership. Since Speaker Cannon was overthrown in 1910, the base of the Speaker's influence has been more informal and personal. This reform need not return the House to the Cannon brand of tyranny, if the motion to call up a bill is privileged and if it may be offered by any member.

A further effect of such a reform, which strengthens the House leadership, could very well be to enhance the powers of Congress vis-à-vis the presidency. The history of the presidency, Professor Edward Corwin has written, is one of aggrandizement, and as Professor David Truman has said, the twentieth century has been hard on national legislatures everywhere.[18] The role of Congress in national decisions has gradually shifted from initiating and originating legislation to legitimating or amending bills sent to it by the executive branch. It is not inconceivable that a centralized and coordinated leadership in the House could be an important step toward strengthening Congress and maintaining the system of checks and balances. Such a prospect should appeal as much to conservatives who have found comfort in

[18] Edward S. Corwin, *The President: Office and Powers, 1787-1957* (New York: New York University Press, 1957, Fourth Revised Edition), pp. 29-30; David B. Truman, *The Congressional Party: A Case Study* (New York: John Wiley and Sons, Inc., 1959), p. 1.

the vetoes of the Rules Committee as to the liberals who have been frustrated by it.

The Committee will not like this alternative, nor will some of its members, perhaps a majority, favor any change. Nor is it at all certain that the recent or contemporary leadership of either party in the House would approve. The late Speaker Rayburn and others have stead-fastly refused to centralize House leadership functions or to formalize informal practices. Rayburn was not nearly as innovative a House leader as Lyndon Johnson was in the Senate, but what he lacked in sanctions he could often compensate for in his uncanny parliamentary skill. And in his later years, in which he became a legend in his own lifetime, he added charisma to skill as a base of power. It is unfor-tunate that he did not formalize more of his power in the Speakership, i.e., that he did not convert his influence into authority.

In certain respects it is misleading to compare Rayburn and other House leaders, for he was so exceptionally able and respected. There will not soon be another like him. But his colleagues and successors apparently share his preference for decentralized authority, which the Speaker can integrate quietly and privately. Hence, there has been resistance to policy committees and other formal instruments of cen-tralized and coordinated leadership. Hence the reluctance of Rayburn and McCormack to reform the Rules Committee as long as Joe Mar-tin was the House Republican leader.

And if the Rules Committee and House leadership are likely to oppose such a proposal, so is the membership of the House. Rules Committee members repeatedly defend their negative decisions by citing the pleas from other members that the Committee protect the House from pressures and embarrassment on particular bills. Judging by the difficulty proponents of change have experienced in obtaining a House majority to discipline the Rules Committee, we may assume that, in general, much of the House approves the Committee's conduct.

Abolition of the Committee would not by itself strengthen Congres-sional independence. It would be only one step toward centralizing House leadership, and it would give impetus to the planning and exe-cution of a coordinated Congressional program, less dependent on the executive branch and more genuinely innovative and creative.

Bibliography

This list of references does not include all items footnoted in the text, but instead is a supplement to an extensive general bibliography on Congress in my *Congress and Foreign Policy-Making: A Study in Legislative Initiative and Influence* (Homewood, Ill.: The Dorsey Press, 1962), pp. 234-53. The following items emphasize general works omitted in or published since the earlier bibliography and particular items on the Committee on Rules.

HEARINGS

Hearings before the Committee on Rules, House of Representatives, Seventy-Ninth Congress, First Session on H.R. 2232 [Discrimination in employment] (Washington: Government Printing Office, 1945).

Hearings before the Committee on Rules, House of Representatives, Eighty-Second Congress, Second Session, on H.R. 7888 and S. 913 [To create a Joint Committee on the Budget] (Washington: Government Printing Office, 1952).

Hearings before the Subcommittee on Legislative Procedure of the Committee on Rules, House of Representatives, Eighty-Third Congress, Second Session, under authority of H. Res. 29 (Washington: Government Printing Office, 1954).

Hearings before a Special Subcommittee of the Committee on Rules, House of Representatives, Eighty-Fourth Congress, Second Session, under authority of H. Res. 462 [To create a standing committee on Administrative Procedure and Practice] (Washington: Government Printing Office, 1956).

Hearings before the Committee on Rules, House of Representatives,

Eighty-Fourth Congress, Second Session, on H.R. 627 [civil rights] (Washington: Government Printing Office, 1956).

Hearings before the Committee on Rules, House of Representatives, Eighty-Fifth Congress, First Session, on H.R. 6127 [civil rights] (Washington: Government Printing Office, 1957).

Hearings before the Joint Committee on the Organization of Congress, Seventy-Ninth Congress, First Session (Washington: Government Printing Office, 1945).

OTHER PUBLICATIONS

Atkinson, Charles R., *The Committee on Rules and the Overthrow of Speaker Cannon* (New York: N.p., 1911).

Bailey, Stephen K., *New Republic,* January 5, 1959.

Beach, Philip F., "Factors Influencing the Decision on a Rule in the House Rules Committee," Unpublished paper, Northwestern University, Political Science D25, 1960.

Berman, Daniel M., *A Bill Becomes a Law: The Civil Rights Act of 1960* (New York: The Macmillan Company, 1962).

Biographical Directory of the American Congress, 1774-1961 (Washington: Government Printing Office, 1961, 85th Cong., 2d Sess., House Doc. 442).

Bolling, Richard, "The House Rules Committee," *University of Missouri Business and Government Review,* 2 (1961), No. 5, 37-45.

Burke, Vincent J., "Federal Spenders Look to 1961," *Nation's Business,* June, 1960, pp. 38-39, 114-18.

Cummings, Milton C., Jr., and Robert L. Peabody, "The Decision to Enlarge the House Rules Committee: An Analysis of the Vote," Mimeographed, July, 1961, and September, 1962.

Dawson, Raymond H., "Congressional Innovation and Intervention in Defense Policy: Legislative Authorization of Weapons Systems," *American Political Science Review,* 56 (1962), 42-57.

Dorough, C. Dwight, *Mr. Sam* (New York: Random House, 1962).

Engel, Irving M., "The Seven Conservatives Who Bottleneck Our Laws," *Reporter,* August 5, 1952, 17-18.

Farmer, Hallie, *The Legislative Process in Alabama* (University, Alabama: Bureau of Public Administration, University of Alabama, 1949).

Fenno, Richard F., Jr., "The House Appropriations Committee as a Political System: The Problem of Integration," *American Political Science Review,* 56 (1962), 310-24.

Froman, Lewis A., "The Importance of Individuality in Voting in Congress," *Journal of Politics,* 25 (1963), 324-32.

_____, "Inter-Party Constituency Differences and Congressional Voting Behavior," *American Political Science Review*, 57 (1963), 57-61.

Galloway, George B., *History of the United States House of Representatives* (Washington: Government Printing Office, 1962, 87th Cong., 1st Sess., House Doc. 246).

_____, (revised by Walter Kravitz), "A Short History of the Development of the House Committee on Rules," Library of Congress, Legislative Reference Service (Mimeographed, 1961).

Goodwin, George, Jr., "Subcommittees: The Miniature Legislatures of Congress," *American Political Science Review*, 56 (1962), 596-604.

Hinderaker, Ivan, "From the 86th to the 87th Congress: Controversy over 'Majority Rule,' " *American Government Annual, 1961-1962* (New York: Holt, Rinehart and Winston, 1961, pp. 76-98).

Hoyt, Mont P., "The House Rules Committee: A Comparative Study of the Change in Membership," Unpublished Honors Paper, Department of Political Science, Northwestern University, 1962.

Jewell, Malcolm, ed., *The Politics of Reapportionment* (New York: Atherton Press 1962).

_____, *The State Legislature—Politics and Practice* (New York: Random House, 1962).

Jones, Charles O., "Representation in Congress: The Case of the House Agriculture Committee," *American Political Science Review*, 55 (1961), 358-67.

"The Keeper of the Rules: Congressman Smith and the New Frontier," (CBS Television Network, January 19, 1961).

Kravitz, Walter, "The Rules Committee Controversy in the 87th Congress: A Brief Resume," Legislative Reference Service, The Library of Congress (Typewritten copy, 1961).

Lapham, Lewis J., *Party Leadership and the House Committee on Rules* (Ph.D. dissertation, Harvard University, 1953).

Lee, Eugene C., *The Presiding Officer and Rules Committee in Legislatures of the United States* (Berkeley: University of California Bureau of Public Administration, 1952).

MacKaye, William R., *A New Coalition Takes Control: The House Rules Committee Fight of 1961* (New York: McGraw-Hill, 1963).

MacNeil, Neil, *Forge of Democracy: The House of Representatives* (New York: David McKay Co., 1963).

McPhee, William N., and William A. Glaser, eds., *Public Opinion and Congressional Elections* (New York: The Free Press of Glencoe, 1962).

MacRae, Duncan, Jr., *Dimensions of Congressional Voting: A Sta-*

tistical Study of the House of Representatives in the Eighty-First Congress (Berkeley: University of California Press, 1958).

Masters, Nicholas A., "Committee Assignments in the House of Representatives," *American Political Science Review,* 55 (1961), 345-57.

Miller, Clem, *Member of the House: Letters of a Congressman,* (ed.) John W. Baker (New York: Charles Scribner's Sons, 1962).

Miller, Warren E., "Majority Rule and the Representative System," Paper prepared for the annual meeting of the American Political Science Association, Washington, D.C., September 5-8, 1962.

————, and Donald E. Stokes, "Policy Preferences of Congressional Candidates and Constituents," Paper prepared for the annual meeting of the American Political Science Association, St. Louis, September 6-9, 1961.

————, and Donald E. Stokes, "Constituency Influence in Congress," *American Political Science Review,* 57 (1963), 45-56.

National Committee for an Effective Congress, *Congressional Report,* 10 (March 4, 1961), No. 1, pp. 1-5.

Norris, George W., *Fighting Liberal: The Autobiography of George W. Norris* (New York: Collier Books, 1961).

Otten, Alan L., "Here's How 12 Men Control Congress," *Nation's Business,* February, 1956, 33 ff.

Peabody, Robert L., "The Committee on Rules and the House Leadership: Some Consequences of Enlargement," *paper delivered at the 1962 annual meeting of the American Political Science Association,* Washington, D. C.

Peabody, Robert L., "The Enlarged Committee on Rules," in Robert L. Peabody and Nelson W. Polsby, *New Perspectives on the House of Representatives* (Chicago: Rand McNally and Co., 1963).

Peek, George, Forthcoming case study of Alaskan Statehood bills, to be published by Inter-University Case Program.

Polsby, Nelson W., "Foreign Policy and Congressional Activity: Or, Can Congress Survive the Solicitude of Its Friends," *World Politics,* 15 (1963), 354-59.

Price, Hugh Douglas, "Race, Religion, and the Rules Committee: The Kennedy Aid-to-Education Bills," in Alan F. Westin, ed., *The Uses of Power: 7 Cases in American Politics* (New York: Harcourt, Brace & World, Inc., 1962), pp. 1-71.

Pringle, Henry F., and Pringle, Katherine, "The 'Terrible Twelve' of Capitol Hill," *Saturday Evening Post,* June 19, 1954, 22 ff.

Radford, Roxanne, "The Rules Committee: Its History, Powers and Functions," Unpublished Washington Semester Project, American University and Beloit College, 1955. On file with the Clerk of the Committee on Rules, House of Representatives.

Riddick, Floyd M., "First Session of the Seventy-Sixth Congress, January 3 to August 5, 1939," *American Political Science Review,* 33 (1939), 1022-43.

————, "Third Session of the Seventy-Sixth Congress, January 3, 1940, to January 3, 1941," *ibid.,* 35 (1941), 284-303.

————, "First Session of the Seventy-Seventh Congress, January 3, 1941, to January 2, 1942," *ibid.,* 36 (1942), 290-302.

————, "Second Session of the Seventy-Seventh Congress," *ibid.,* 37 (1943), 290-305.

————, "The First Session of the Seventy-Eighth Congress," *ibid.,* 38 (1944), 301-17.

————, "The Second Session of the Seventy-Eighth Congress," *ibid.,* 39 (1945), 317-36.

————, "The First Session of the Seventy-Ninth Congress," *ibid.,* 40 (1946), 256-71.

————, "The Second Session of the Seventy-Ninth Congress," *ibid.,* 41 (1947), 12-27.

————, "The First Session of the Eightieth Congress," *ibid.,* 42 (1948), 677-93.

————, "The Second Session of the Eightieth Congress," *ibid.,* 43 (1949), 483-92.

————, "The Eighty-First Congress: First and Second Sessions," *Western Political Quarterly,* 4 (1951), 48-67.

————, "The Eighty-Second Congress: First Session," *ibid.,* 5 (1952), 94-108.

————, "The Eighty-Second Congress: Second Session," *ibid.,* 5 (1952), 619-34.

————, "The Eighty-Third Congress: First Session," *ibid.,* 6 (1953), 776-94.

————, "The Eighty-Third Congress: Second Session," *ibid.,* 7 (1954), 636-55.

————, "The Eighty-Fourth Congress: First Session," *ibid.,* 8 (1955), 612-29.

————, "The Eighty-Fourth Congress: Second Session," *ibid.,* 10 (1957), 49-62.

————, "The Eighty-Fifth Congress: First Session," *ibid.,* 11 (1958), 86-103.

————, "The Eighty-Fifth Congress: Second Session," *ibid.,* 12 (1959), 177-92.

Riker, William H., and Donald Niemi, "The Stability of Coalitions on Roll Calls in the House of Representatives," *American Political Science Review*, 56 (1962), 58-65.

Robinson, James A., *Decision-Making in the Committee on Rules* (Ph.D. dissertation, Northwestern University, 1957, Ann Arbor: University Microfilms, Mic. 58-4423). [It was the first draft of this book.]

————, "Decision-making in the House Rules Committee" *Administrative Science Quarterly*, 3 (1958), 73-86. [A confusing piece, best left forgotten.]

————, "The Role of the Rules Committee in Arranging the Program of the U. S. House of Representatives," *Western Political Quarterly*, 12 (1959), 653-669. [Parts are incorporated and updated in Chapter 2, but one or two unpromising analyses are dropped.]

————, "Coming Conflict over the House Rules Committee," *The Progressive*, December, 1960, 29-33. [The principal policy recommendation and reform alternatives are incorporated in Chapter 6.]

————, "The Role of the Rules Committee in Regulating Debate in the U. S. House of Representatives," *Midwest Journal of Political Science*, 5 (1961), 59-69. [Updated and included in Chapter 3.]

————, "Organizational and Constituency Backgrounds of the House Rules Committee," in Joseph R. Fiszman, ed., *The American Political Arena* (Boston: Little, Brown & Co., 1962), pp. 211-18. [Brought up to date, revised, and extended in Chapter 5.]

————, "History and Powers of the House Committee on Rules," American Enterprise Institute Legislative Analysis Series, 1963. [Part of Chapter 4.]

Schubert, Glendon A., Jr., "The Twenty-one Day Rule: The Politics of Legislative Procedure," *Political Science*, 5 (1953), 16-29.

Smith, A. Robert, *The Tiger in the Senate: The Biography of Wayne Morse* (Garden City: Doubleday and Company, Inc., 1962).

Swanstrom, Roy, *The United States Senate, 1787-1801: A Dissertation on the First Fourteen Years of the Upper Legislative Body* (Washington: Government Printing Office, 1962, 87th Cong., 1st Sess., Senate Doc. No. 64).

Swearer, Howard R., "The Controversy over 'Backdoor Financing in the 86th Congress,' First Session," Unpublished ms., 1961.

Van Hollen, Christopher, *The House Committee on Rules (1933-1951): Agent of Party and Agent of Opposition* (Ph.D. dissertation, The Johns Hopkins University, 1951).

Wahlke, John C., Heinz Eulau, William Buchanan, LeRoy C. Ferguson, *The Legislative System: Explorations in Legislative Behavior* (New York: John Wiley and Sons, Inc., 1962).

White, William S., "The Invisible Gentleman from Kansas City [Richard Bolling]," *Harper's,* May 1961, pp. 83-87.

Wicker, Tom, "Again That Roadblock in Congress," *New York Times Magazine,* August 7, 1960, pp. 14, 64, 68.

Williamson, Willard F., "House Rules Committee: An Appraisal," *Social Order,* February 1962.

Young, Roland, *The British Parliament* (London and Evanston: Faber and Faber and Northwestern University Press, 1962).

Index

Agriculture, Committee on, 49, 94, 97
Alexander, DeAlva Stanwood, 59*n*
Alien Registration Act (1940), 13, 83
Allen, Leo, 68, 82, 88, 98
Appropriations Committee, 32, 94, 95, 96, 97
  limitations imposed on, 47-51
Avery, William, 80

Bankhead, Speaker William, 81
Banking and Currency, Committee on, 94, 95, 97
  bargaining with Rules Committee, 31-32
  during investigation of OPA, 37-40
Bargaining, 112
Bolling, Richard, 98, 99
Boudinot, Elias, 59
Brown, Clarence, 13-14, 69, 88, 98
Bruck, H. W., 89*n*
Buchanan, Frank, 104
Buchanan, William, 123*n*
Budge, Hamer, 85, 95, 101
Burdette, Franklin L., 111*n*

Burns, James McGregor, 2*n*, 17-18
Byrd, Harry, 83
Calendar Wednesday, 7, 8-9, 11, 12, 60, 69-70
Cannon, Clarence, 50, 50*n*, 58*n*, 84
Cannon, Joseph G., 58, 66, 71, 126
  revolt against, 60-62
Cannonism, 71, 78
  defeat of, 60-62
  (*see also* Rules, Committee on, organization of)
Carlisle, John G., 59
Carroll, Holbert N., 1*n*, 16-17, 95*n*
Case, Francis, 29
Celler, Emmanuel, 13-14
Childs, Marquis, 39
Civil Rights Commission, 18-19
Civil rights legislation, 13, 18-19, 51-52, 67, 85
Clark, J. Bayard, 96
Closed rule, 11, 54
  controversial nature of, 46
  definition of, 43-44
  "gag" rule, 44-45
  logrolling, 44
  (*see also* Rules, Committee on)
Cochran, John J., 37

Colmer, William, 52, 67, 72, 77, 85, 100, 105
Committees, Committee on, 115
Consent Calendar, 3-5, 7-8, 9, 60
Cooper, Jere, 104
Corwin, Edward S., 126
Cox, Eugene, 17, 31, 45, 64, 65, 67, 67n, 69
Cummings, Milton C., Jr., 78n

Dahl, Robert A., 95, 112n
Debating time estimated, 53-54
Delaney, James, 80, 92, 99, 103
Dies, Martin, 99
Discharge Calendar, 4-6, 7, 9, 33, 60
Discharge Petition, 12, 33, 113
  bringing legislation to floor, 4-6
  differences between 21-Day Rule, 69-70
  used against Rules Committee, 17-18
District of Columbia, Committee on, 7, 9, 94, 97
Donovan, Robert J., 91n
Dorough, C. Dwight, 78n
Douglas, Paul, 90
Driver, William J., 92, 96
Dulles, Allen, 81

Eberhart, John C., 94-95
Eberharter, Herman P., 41, 68
Education and Labor, Committee on, 17, 97
  and opposition to FEPC, 64, 71
  criticism of Rules Committee, 29
  denied rules to education bills, 18, 80
Eisenhower, Dwight D., 77, 82
Eleazer, Frank, 84n
Elliott, Carl, 80, 92, 96, 100

Ellsworth, Harris, 49
Emergency Price Control Act (1942), 37
Eulau, Heinz, 123n

Farnsworth, David N., 1n
Federal Pay Raise Act (1960), 5, 33
Feighan, Michael, 104
Fenno, Richard F., Jr., 1n
Fenton, John, 100
Ferguson, Leroy C., 123n
Filibuster, 111
Fish, Hamilton, 36, 39, 93-94, 96
Five-minute rule, 44
  (see also Open rule)
Foreign Affairs Committee, 94, 95, 96, 97

Galloway, George B., 2n, 94n, 123
  on proposed reforms of Rules Committee, 116-18
George, Walter, 83
Gerry, Elbridge, 59
Goodwin, George, Jr., 111n
Graves, Audrey, 84n
Green, Edith, 79
Gwinn, William R., 61-62

Halleck, Charles, 69, 70, 72, 77, 96, 97-98
Harlan, Byron, 96
Hart, Edward J., 104
Hechler, Kenneth W., 61-62, 61n
Hedrick, E. H., 104
Heller, Louis, 68
Henry, Patrick, 83
Herblock, 20, 73, 76, 124
Herter, Christian, 69, 93, 96
Hinds, Asher, 58n, 59n

Holcombe, Arthur N., 61*n*
House Calendar, 3-5
Huitt, Ralph K., 90*n*
Hyneman, Charles S., 112*n*, 115*n*

Immigration and Naturalization, Committee on, 94, 97
Insurgent Republicans, 60-62
Interior and Insular Affairs, Committee on, 25, 28, 97
Interstate and Foreign Commerce Committee, 94, 95, 97

Jefferson, Thomas, 83
Johnson, Lyndon B., 77, 127
Jones, Charles O., 1*n*
Judiciary, Committee on, 13-15, 94, 97

Kaplan, Abraham, 10*n*, 17
Karsten, Frank, 104
Kefauver, Estes, 77
Kendall, Willmoore, 99*n*
Kennedy, John F., 75, 77, 104
Key, V. O., 100
Korea, 41

La Follette, Robert, 90
Lapham, Lewis, 67*n*, 116
  on proposed reforms of Rules Committee, 118-20
Lasswell, Harold D., 10*n*, 17
Latham, Henry J., 99
Lee, Robert E., 83
Lesinski, John, 71
Lindblom, Charles E., 112*n*
Luce, Robert, 35*n*, 116
Lyle, John, 67*n*, 96

McClean, Donald, 96
McCormack, John, 7, 58, 82, 104, 105, 127

McCormack, John (cont.)
  interpretation of 21-Day Rule, 70
MacNeil, Neil, 78*n*
MacRae, Duncan, Jr., 100
McSweeney, John, 92
Madden, Ray, 52, 64, 105*n*
Madison, James, 59, 83
"Majority rule," 65-68
Mansfield, Mike, 104
Mapes, Carl, 93
Marcantonio, Vito, 64
Marshall, John, 83
Martin, Joseph W., 58, 82, 91, 96, 97
  association with Rayburn, 72, 77, 127
Masters, Nicholas A., 94
Michener, Earl, 94
Mills, Wilbur, 41
Moley, Raymond, 84*n*
Monroe, James, 83
Monroney, Mike, 67-68
Morgan, Dr. Thomas, 104
Motivations of congressmen, 90-92
Murdock, Victor, 61

Nixon, Richard M., 75, 77
Norms, 5-6, 8, 90-91
  external, 6
  internal, 5-6
Norris, George, 58, 58*n*, 90
Norton, Mrs. Mary, 28-29

Objectors, Committee of, 4, 9
O'Connor, John J., 35, 81, 83, 92
Open rule, 11, 54
  definition of, 44
  "five-minute rule," 44
  pro forma amendments, 44
  waivers added to, 46
  (*see also* Rules, Committee on)

Otten, Alan L., 2*n*

Peabody, Robert L., 15*n*, 19, 78*n*
Peek, George, 87
Personal characteristics of
    congressmen, 90-92
Peterson, Hardin, 71
Political Parties, Committee on, 114
Polyarchy, 112
Post Office, Committee on, 94, 95,
    97
Pou, Edward, 81
Powell, Adam Clayton, 77, 79
Price Administration, Office of, 37
Pringle, Henry F. and Katherine, 2*n*
Private Calendar, 3-5, 9
Public Lands, Committee on, 71, 97
Public Works, Committee on, 28,
    97

Railway Labor Act, 35
Rainey, Henry, 82
Ranney, Austin, 99*n*, 111*n*
Rayburn, Sam, 41, 50*n*, 52, 58, 67*n*,
    75, 81, 82, 84, 90
    on enlarging Rules Committee,
        77-78
    on party unity, 103-5
    on price control extension, 39-40
    opposing suspension of the
        rules, 7
    parliamentary skill of, 127
    supporting social welfare legisla-
        tion, 72
    supporting 21-Day Rule, 67
Reams, Frazier, 65
Reorganization Act (1946), 58, 111
    (*see also* Rules, Committee on,
        organization of)
Revision of Laws, Committee on,
    96, 97

Riddick, Floyd M., 2*n*, 4*n*, 5, 9,
    35*n*, 36*n*, 37, 101*n*
Riesman, David, 16
Rizley, Ross, 93
Robinson, James A., 10*n*, 19*n*, 102*n*
Roosevelt, Franklin D., 18, 81, 83
Rules, Committee on
    as arbiter, 30-33, 51-53
    the Calendars, 3-6
    chairman's power in, 84-88
    closed and open rules, 11, 43-46
    decisions of, 62
        cross-party votes, 107-9
        straight-party votes, 105-7
    foreign/domestic policy, 16-18
    hearings denied, 23-25
    'horse-trading' in, 14
    legislative days, 6-10
    liberal/conservative views, 19
    members of
        bipartisan unity scores, 107-9
        constituency background, 98-
            103
        influence on public policy,
            103-9
        organizational experience, 92-
            98
        party unity scores, 105-7
        previous committee assign-
            ments, 94-98
        prior congressional service,
            92-94
        region, 99-101
        safe-competitive districts,
            102-3
        states represented, 98-99
        urban—rural districts,
            101-2
    organization of
        Cannonism, 60-62

Rules, Committee on (*cont.*)
  organization of (*cont.*)
    origins and early growth, 58-60
    "packing," 71-80
    Reorganization Act (1946), 58, 111
    21-Day Rule, 63-71
  powers of
    bases, 10-12
    extent
      domain, 19-21
      scope, 16-19
      weight, 15-16
    means, 12-15
  proposed reforms
    legislative independence, 121-26
      doctrine defined, 112-13
      obstacle to, 113
    party responsibility, 114-21
      doctrine defined, 111-12
  regulating debating time, 53-55
  rules denied, 25-30
  usurpation of prerogatives of other committees, 37
  waivers of point of order
    limitations of, 47, 50-51
    objections to, 48-51
    reasons for, 47-48

Sabath, Adolph, 93-94, 103-4
  arbitrating Rules Committee conflicts, 30-32
  on allocating time, 24
  on limiting waivers against points of order, 47-48
  on the 21-Day Rule, 64-67
  record as Rules Committee chairman, 81-82, 120-21
St. George, Katherine, 93

Sapin, Burton, 89*n*
Schlesinger, Arthur M., Jr., 121*n*
Scott, Hugh, 52
Seniority system, 111
Sherman, Roger, 59
Sisk, B.J., 80, 101
Slaughter, Roger, 92, 99
Smith, A. Robert, 90*n*
Smith-Connally Labor Act, 83
Smith, H. Allen, 101
Smith, Howard W., 17, 49*n*, 50*n*, 52, 67, 72, 77, 79, 98, 100, 121
  background of, 82-84
  chairman of committee investigating OPA, 37-40
  dissatisfaction of Rules Committee members with, 74-75
  on limiting use of closed rule, 45
  opposing "judicial invasion," 13-14
  record as Rules Committee chairman, 84-88
Snyder, Richard C., 89*n*
Special orders, 59
Spence, Brent, 40-41
Standing, William H., 102*n*
Steiner, Gilbert Y., 1*n*
Stevenson, Adlai, 77
Stigler, William, 104
Supreme Court, 13
Suspension of the rules, 7,11
  votes necessary for, 4

Taber, John, 48-49
Taylor, J. Will, 37, 93
Taylor, Zachary, 83
Thornberry, Homer, 100, 108
Tillett, Paul, 91*n*
Trimble, James, 80, 88, 92, 100, 108

Truman, David B., 82n, 126
Truman, Harry S, 34, 63, 99
21-Day Rule, 34, 113, 117
  effects of, 69-71
  reasons for, 63-68
  repeal of, 65
  (*see also* Rules, Committee on, organization of)

Unanimous consent agreements, 3, 8, 11, 19
Union Calendar, 3-4
U.S. House of Representatives
  bills and resolutions presented to, 2-3
  controversial bills in, 10
  foreign policy-making in, 16
  reviewing Rules Committee decisions, 33-41
U.S. Treasury, 32

Van Hollen, Christopher, 36, 118n

Veterans Affairs, Committee on, 28, 95, 97

Wadsworth, James, 69, 92
Wage and Hour Act (1938), 5, 17, 33
Wahlke, John C., 123n
Washington, George, 83
Ways and Means Committee, 94, 95, 96, 97, 115
  forced to act by Rules Committee, 13, 29, 41
West, W. Reed, 121-22
White, William S., 52n, 70
Whole, Committee of the, 1
Wicker, Tom, 75n
Wilson, Woodrow, 2, 60, 116

Young, Roland, 37n, 115n

Zeller, Belle, 114n